Canadian Accountant's

Guide to the

INTERNET

Second Edition

DONALD E. SHEEHY, CA
GERALD D. TRITES, FCA

CARSWELL
Thomson Professional Publishing

Canadian Cataloguing in Publication Data

Sheehy, Donald E.
    Canadian accountant's guide to the Internet

2nd ed.
Includes index.
ISBN 0-459-57642-9

1. Accounting – Computer network resources. 2. Internet (Computer network).   I. Trites, Gerald. II. Title.

HF5625.7.S53 1998   025.06′657   C98-932291-2

 The paper used in this publication meets the minimum requirements of American National Standard for Information Sciences — Permanence of Paper for Printed Library Material, ANSI Z39.48-1984.

CARSWELL
Thomson Professional Publishing

One Corporate Plaza, 2075 Kennedy Road, Scarborough, Ontario M1T 3V4
Customer Service:
Toronto 1-416-609-3800
Elsewhere in Canada/U.S. 1-800-387-5164
Fax 1-416-298-5904

TABLE OF CONTENTS

PART TWO: INTERNET SOURCES

6. FINANCE AND THE WEB 77

7. GOVERNMENT AND TAXATION 101

8. INFORMATION TECHNOLOGY 119

9. BUSINESS MANAGEMENT

10. EDUCATION

LIST OF FIGURES

FOREWORD

WELCOME TO OUR SECOND EDITION

In the short 12-month period since our first edition was published, the Internet has more than doubled in size. At March 1998, the WWW was estimated to comprise 275 million pages. Based on the analysis by Digital Equipment, the WWW had again doubled in nine months and continues to grow at a rate of 20 million pages per month. One of the most notable increases has been in new business sites, due to the increased use of the Internet for developing business and electronic commerce settlement.

The needs of accountants for information are as diversified as the work they do. Accountants work in several sectors in our society, including public practice, industry, government, and academia. They work alone, in partnerships, in big organizations, and in small ones. This diversity complicates the task of analyzing the needs of accountants for information from the Internet.

Despite these varied environments, several commonalities stand out. For example, we can assume that accountants are interested in accounting issues. Since many of them are in management positions, they are interested in information about management issues and techniques. They are usually interested in legislation, especially tax and regulatory legislation. In addition, they often have a need for information about finance, investing, information technology, auditing, and the profession in general.

Accountants are busy business people and, although surfing the Net can make great entertainment, like most business people, they simply do not have the time. In business, people need relevant information and they need it fast. Accountants are no different. For this reason, the vast array of information on the Internet is often not available to accountants when they need it. The purpose of this book is to help them to find a fast route to the information they need on the Internet without spending a lot of time searching for it.

The Internet can be an effective business tool, but it requires a knowledge of those sites that contain needed information or lead to those that do. The number of Web sites dealing with the subject matters covered here are indeed staggering. The easy route would be to simply catalogue as many of them as possible. However, we have taken the more difficult approach of attempting to identify those which have the most relevant and concrete information likely to be of use to accountants. In a sense, we have opted for quality over quantity. Most accountants in Canada will find the sites we have mentioned in this book satisfy a majority of their needs.

This book will be useful for any accountant who is interested in using the Internet but doesn't want to spend a lot of time learning how, or doesn't have the time for aimless searching for information. It is generally, but not exclusively, directed to business purposes. It provides a brief background on the Internet, including various technical considerations. It features the accounting and business related resources available and provides a practical guide to making use of those resources. Finally, we offer a summary of the best Web sites available for accountants and the specific addresses (URLs) where they can be found.

We know that purchasers of this guide will find it useful. But we also know that, like fine wine, it can improve with age, but this will only be possible if we receive the experiences and suggestions of our readers. Any comments on this second edition would be most appreciated and can be emailed to *dsheehy@idirect.com* or *gtrites@stfx.ca.*

INTRODUCTION

This book has been designed to supply general information on the Internet to provide assistance to navigate the Net effectively, and to provide sources from which the accountant can get *relevant* information. The last few chapters address more futuristic types of issues.

Part One: Essentials on Information

Chapter 1 Welcome to the "Net"

This introductory chapter discusses various background issues on the Internet, such as what is the Internet and why an accountant might want to use it.

Chapter 2 Navigating the World Wide Web

This chapter discusses the popular search engines and how to do an effective search on the WWW section of the Internet (which is the primary focus of this guide).

Chapter 3 Other Sections of the Net

Chapter 3 focuses on email, mailing lists and how to retrieve information from newsgroups. It also shows how to use some of the other portions of the Internet that are less popular, but can sometimes be useful.

Part Two: Internet Sources

Chapter 4 Accounting and Financial Reporting

As the chapter name implies, this chapter concentrates on the vast number of accounting and financial reporting sites that are available on the Internet. It also addresses the use of the Internet by corporations as a vehicle for publishing their annual financial and other information.

Chapter 5 Assurance Services

This chapter addresses the move to assurance services by practitioners and addresses significant external and internal auditing sites that can be now located on the WWW. It also addresses public sector auditing.

Chapter 6 Finance and the Web

Chapter 6 discusses how the accountant can use the Internet for financial information. Although this chapter focuses on specific information sites, it does provide some guidance on how to get information on financial concepts. Specific information is provided on business news sites, investment research, banks, trust companies and credit unions as well as mutual funds and financial planners.

Chapter 7 Government and Taxation

This chapter provides a significant amount of information on federal, provincial, territorial and municipal government sites and focuses on tax information and software sites. There is also a brief discussion on government grants.

Chapter 8 Information Technology

Chapter 8 discusses how the accountant can use the Internet to resource information technology. The chapter covers areas such as hardware sales and support, application software, auditing and accounting software, security, and computer literature sites.

Chapter 9 Business Management

Popular business management and project management sites in Canada and abroad are discussed in Chapter 9. It also discusses sites for business news and management research.

Chapter 10 Education

This chapter discusses Canadian educational sites of universities, community colleges, schools and distance education.

Chapter 11 Regulatory/Currency/Trade Information

Sites regulating the various industries in Canada, including the Government of Canada, Securities Commissions, Trade Commissions and so on are addressed in this chapter. It also addresses popular sites that can be accessed for currency informa-

tion. These are in addition to those discussed in Chapter 5.

Chapter 12 Securities Information

Chapter 12 provides extensive information on Canadian securities, including the exchanges and where to get investment information and advice.

Part Three: Current Developments

Chapter 13 Electronic Commerce on the Web

This chapter focuses on the growing use of the Internet for electronic commerce, especially for transactional purposes. It also discusses the use of intranets and extranets and how they relate to the use of the Web by organizations. The last part of the chapter addresses one of the most crucial issues, security of data on the Net, as well as the ongoing threat of hacking into corporate sites.

Chapter 14 Financial Reporting on the Web

Chapter 14 explores the use of the Web for financial reporting and provides a number of examples of sites providing financial information and sites that catalogue sources of corporate annual reports.

You will notice that we have continued to avoid what many Internet books do, that is, provide pages and pages of filler material, such as the names of all 15,000+ newsgroups that can easily add over 30 pages to a book. We have also kept screen shot illustrations to a minimum, showing only what we believe to be the key sites in each area. In doing so, we have tried to make sure that the reader gets as much relevant information as possible, while avoiding what is likely to be extraneous.

1 WELCOME TO THE "NET"

INTRODUCTION

We are assuming that you have recently signed on to the Internet (the "Net"), quite simply, the world's largest network. Having established your connection, you have passed through that electronic toll-booth and have joined over 80 million North American users on the *information highway*. How fast or slow that you travel on your route will depend on a number of factors (including both hardware and software), one of the most important of which is a working knowledge of tips and information on how to make your trips effective and efficient.

To get to this starting gate, we are assuming that you already have the necessary hardware and software (or you could easily acquire in off-the-shelf Internet-oriented solutions). The more important factor is attainable through a working knowledge of Internet management, requiring first hand experience and specialized knowledge of how the Internet could be effectively used in your particular environment. It is in this area where this book will prove to be of great assistance.

The book is designed to focus on a significant professional user group—accountants. It is designed to be a useful guide for those conducting their own practice as well as those in government or business. The approach that this book takes is to focus on the needs of accountants and then to show how the Internet can be used to assist with or satisfy those needs. The book also deals with how the Internet can be used to obtain information about essential business information, like markets, regulatory environments, and the competition.

The reader will gain clear understandable guidance and precise information about specific homepages of relevance. The information provided should enable accountants to assess what specifically needed information might be available, access that information and bookmark it for future reference. The focus is on the use of the Internet as an essential business tool—how it can fit into the daily functional needs of an accounting user.

First of all, we've assumed you've already become connected, either through the organization that you work for, or through an independent Internet service provider (ISP). If you have not reached this stage yet, the Table at the end of this chapter has some hints on how to choose an ISP.

FOCUS OF THIS GUIDE

This book focuses on how an accountant can effectively use the Internet. We are not orienting this towards the Internet power user, rather someone who has a basic familiarity and wants to be able to access the Internet to acquire additional knowledge in accounting, auditing, finance or other business or operational areas.

Quite frankly, there are hundreds of books that have been written on Internet basics, with little progression beyond providing the reader with what is the Internet, what are the sections of the Internet (WWW, user groups, etc.), how to connect to the Internet, and so on. Few have been written with the more serious user in mind. Even fewer have been written to address how the Internet can be used to assist specific professions. It is for that reason we are reaching to a higher level of user.

THE INTERNET EXPLAINED

Quite simply, the Internet is the world's largest computer network, using a network of networks to link over 60 million people. We say "over" as it is impossible to estimate what an accurate measure might be.

It is not controlled by any particular company or country. It began as a US defense department initiative some 25 years ago. Its major purpose at that time was to facilitate military message transfers between computers. Although it did experience some growth in the 1970s and 1980s, its real growth began in 1993 when the World Wide Web (WWW) section of In-

ternet became popular with the release of the MOSAIC browser. Since then its growth has been astronomical. For example, five years ago there were only a few WWW sites, and relatively few users. Now it is estimated that there are over 5 million computers in use with some 18 million WWW sites now available. During the first few years, the WWW was believed to double every 53 days, and its intense growth will likely continue into the foreseeable future, although this rate of growth is bound to level off. At March 1998, the WWW was estimated to comprise 275 million pages. Based on the analysis by Digital Equipment, the WWW had again doubled in nine months and continues to grow at a rate of 20 million pages per month, a significant growth rate.

With its massive growth and the introduction of GUI interface-based browser software, the Internet has become the most influential communication system that currently exists. It has caused a unique global revolution in the manner in which information can be distributed facilitating transfers between remote computers at breathtaking speeds.

- It is now the world's biggest email system, allowing messages and files to be sent anywhere in the world without incurring any long distance charges. It has become the backbone for Canadian business email systems, facilitating direct access between a company (and its employees) and potential customers anywhere in the world. As will be discussed later, various organizations are now providing free Internet email through their sites.

- It has created a new service industry through the Internet service provider (ISP) who provides easy connection gateways for individuals and businesses to the Internet for browsing access, email, or to facilitate and maintain WWW pages for customers.

- It is the WWW. This part of the Web has been responsible for its significant growth, allowing easy access through point and click software to Web pages that contain text, graphics, and even sound, music and movie clips. All WWW sites have specific, unique addresses called URLs (uniform resource locators).

- It's the world's biggest information service, much useful, much useless. The Internet contains much free information made available by governments, universities, and corporations and now has recently become a significant public relations vehicle by corporations. The real challenge is to efficiently traverse this massive storehouse of knowledge to effectively gain the information sought. WWW "surfing" can be fun, but is usually very inefficient.

- It is a significant world wide marketplace to sell product or information services. The potential for electronic commerce over the Net will increase dramatically once consumers are assured that transactional and other information will be well protected.

- It is a financial settlement medium, as organizations begin to offer more and

more electronic commerce services online. There is the potential to avoid using cheques to settle routine bills and other charges.

- It is providing a mechanism for inexpensive electronic meetings, now also providing the ability to conduct low-level video conferencing between individuals anywhere in the world using local call rates.

- It is a common computer platform using standard communication protocols. Because it allows the use of standard tools regardless of the technology platform, it has spawned a new breed of networks, intranets and extranets (these are discussed later in Chapter 13).

Although it is the largest network, there is no government or organization that controls the Internet, although many organizations are trying to censor Internet content. Despite efforts of some foreign governments at controlling the Internet, most notably the United States, it remains a truly distributed network under no central authority.[1] The Internet itself has some organizations that act as coordinators, such as InterNIC at *http://rs.internic.net*, that maintains the national registry of Internet domain names and owners. Otherwise, all responsibilities for

---

[1] For example, on July 23, 1998, the US Senate approved the first legislation restricting content on the Internet since portions of the *Communications Decency Act* were ruled unconstitutional by the Supreme Court in summer 1997. However, the House has yet to vote on its own version of the legislation. The two chambers of Congress would have to resolve any differences before sending the bill to President Clinton. Even then, it would likely face significant challenge in the courts.

support and network services are distributed worldwide.

WHY SHOULD ACCOUNTANTS USE THE INTERNET?

POPULARITY AND CHALLENGES

Why should accountants use the Internet? First of all, their clients are becoming major Internet users. In order to effectively service them, it is important that accountants be technologically literate. That literacy now includes the Internet. In addition, cyberspace has introduced a whole range of new issues. Finally, the Internet, properly used, can provide the accountant with a number of new effective tools.

Let's deal with the Internet's popularity. Only a few years ago, the Internet was the domain of early technology "nerds". In five years it became the mainstream link to the information highway around the world. The landscape of the Internet has also changed quickly. Online services, such as America Online (AOL), CompuServe, and others have made connecting to the Internet easy for one and all. In fact, America Online is regarded as the largest ISP in the United States.

As a result, businesses are embracing the Internet, using it for product promotion, email, general and targeted information, and recently, for electronic commerce. They have passed that stage where they have to look at the business sense for having a WWW site; their competition likely has one and, in order to survive in this global marketplace, they need one too. They are beginning to provide information that could be more sensitive on their sites (for example, specific financial information) that unknown users might rely on in hopes of attracting more business. This has its challenges for accountants.

CLIENT EXPECTATIONS

The Internet will continue to force accountants to a new technological horizon. As clients become more Net-aware, it will be important for the accountant to invest in this resource in order to advise and communicate with the client. For example, the client might want the accountant to be on email to facilitate seamless communication—at any hour of any day. The client may want to solicit advice as to the hazards of exterior network access, and the reasons for firewalls. It will be important that the accountant be able to provide sufficient advice. In addition, clients may request assurance as to the security on a particular Internet site. These and other assurance and consulting services will continue to develop as the use of the Internet grows and the client's use becomes more sophisticated.

Unfortunately, the accounting profession is not normally proactive, and is generally risk adverse. In technology, however, the profession may not be able to take years to develop standards based on proven methodologies. Time, and other consulting competitors, might pass us by if we are too conservative in developing approaches to dealing with the Internet and the uses it presents. The accountant will lose his or her position as a key adviser to the client on business systems and the opening field of electronic commerce.

RESOURCES

This book will focus on discussing the resources that the Internet offers. As you will see, the Internet has boundless information that could be relevant for the accountant. It offers email, hardware and software support, and information on all facets of an accountant's work (taxation,

accounting, assurance, and so on). The Internet will prove to be the most influential force on business over the next few years, and as a result, could have a significant impact on the accountant.

MARKETING POTENTIAL

The Internet offers the potential for marketing an accountant's business and for developing new services (as we have recently seen with the introduction of WebTrust by the Canadian Institute of Chartered Accountants and The American Institute of Certified Public Accountants). It offers the potential for rapid feedback.

Since many publications have already been written on how to market or expand your business on the Internet, we will not address this area in this book.

Finding a Suitable Internet Service Provider (ISP)

The following are some of the areas that you should research before signing up with an ISP.

- **Cost.** Cost usually starts very low— $9.95 is common, but this is for a minimum number of hours before a high surcharge per hour is billed. Initial surfing usually can take a large amount of time, therefore it is important to have a sufficient number of hours included in the monthly fixed fee. Beware of low-cost unlimited access sites. These can be too popular and access can be difficult due to the sheer number of subscribers. The most vivid example of this was in late 1996/early 1997 when America Online experienced significant growth due to a promotion of 50 free hours' access, a growth that overwhelmed its systems and angered a great number of its existing subscribers.

- **Access.** It is important to check the ISP's assertion about subscriber ability to get access to the system. This involves a number of issues, including number of subscribers, number of lines and overall maintenance of the site. It is also important that the ISP has high-speed line modem access (currently 56KB). The faster the modem's access, the better.

- **Training.** Ideally, the ISP should supply training material or training sessions on Internet basics.

- **Software and Support.** The ISP should provide, free-of-charge, all of the software that is needed to get you running on the Internet. All of the popular browsers, newsreaders, etc., are usually free. The ISP should also have a toll-free line and generous amount of hours available daily for user support.

- **Toll-free Numbers or Multi-Locations.** Many corporate computer users, and accountants are certainly no exception, use their computers from remote sites. These could be in the same city, or it could be a different province or country. In order to provide the highest level of usability, it is important that the ISP either have multi-locations or have a toll-free number to dial into. In this way, expensive long distance charges can be avoided. This is one of the big advantages of services such as CompuServe that have a local number almost everywhere in North America and abroad.

2 NAVIGATING THE WORLD WIDE WEB

INTRODUCTION

The World Wide Web segment of the Internet now comprises in excess of 300 million pages and 15 billion words. In addition, there are in excess of 15,000 newsgroups that deal with a variety of moderated and non-moderated topics. Unless a person knows of a particular URL address, they will not be able to effectively surf the Internet for information. Most people just don't have the time to find all the useful information out there by surfing. The alternative is to do effective searches for specific information on the significant sections of the Internet.

This means the would-be Internet surfer must become a dedicated user of the sophisticated search engines and other programs that have been created to navigate the Web. That's the only way to make effective use of this significant electronic resource. This chapter discusses ways to effectively navigate the Net for accounting and related information.

SEARCHING THE WWW SECTION

WHAT ARE SEARCH ENGINES AND HOW DO THEY WORK?

First of all, you need to use a search engine. Search engines use software robots to survey the Web and build their databases. Web documents are retrieved and indexed. When you enter a query at a search engine WWW site, your input is checked against that search engine's keyword indices. The best matches are then returned to you as "hits".

KEYWORD INDEXING

There are two primary methods of text indexing—keyword and concept. Keyword indexing is the most common form of text indexing on the Web and is used by most search engines. Unless the author of the Web document specifies the keywords for the document, it's up to the search engine to determine what the keywords should be. Essentially, this means that search engines pull out words that are thought to be significant. Words that are mentioned towards the top of a document and words that are repeated several times throughout the document are more likely to be deemed important.

Keyword searches have a tough time distinguishing between words that are spelled the same, but mean something different (e.g., capital assets, capital punishment, capital contributions). This often results in hits that are completely irrelevant to your query. Consider the words "debit" and "credit". Debit will appear in debit cards and a few other non-accounting sites. Credit will appear in a number of situations such as movie and song credits. Some search engines also have trouble with so-called stemming, that is, if you enter the word "large", should they return a hit on the word, "larger"? There are also problems with singular and plural words and verb tenses that differ from the word you entered by only an "s", or an "ed".

Search engines also cannot return hits on keywords that mean the same, but are not actually entered in your query. A query on fixed assets would not return a document that used the word "capital" instead of "fixed".

Concept-Based Indexing

Unlike keyword indexed-based systems, concept-based indexing systems try to determine what you really mean, not just what you enter. Essentially, they do this by checking documents for dominant themes or concepts, which are then indexed. A concept-based search returns hits on documents that are about the subject/theme you're exploring, even if the words in the document don't precisely match the words you enter into the query.

Excite is currently the best-known search engine site on the WWW that uses concept-based searching.

How does concept-based searching work? There are various methods of building concept-based indices. Some are very complex, relying on sophisticated linguistic and artificial intelligence theory. Others, such as excite, use a numerical approach. It determines meaning by calculating the frequency with which certain important words appear. When several words or phrases that are tagged to signal a particular concept appear close to each other in a text, the search engine concludes, by statistical analysis, that the piece is "about" a certain subject.

The results are best when you enter a lot of words, all of which roughly refer to the concept for which you're seeking information. Concept-based indexing is a good idea, but it's far from perfect.

Pick Your Engine

The Web is potentially a terrific place to get information on almost any topic. Doing research without leaving your desk sounds like a great idea, but all too often you end up wasting precious time chasing down what turn out to be useless URLs. Eventually, there will be an easy way to do effective and efficient searches. For the time being, however, the user needs to test the various engines that are available and decide which ones best suit their particular needs.

It's important to give some thought to your search strategy. Are you just beginning to accumulate knowledge on a broad subject? Or do you have a specific objective, such as finding out everything you can about a specific auditing problem or accounting issue.

If you're more interested in broad, general information, the first place to go to is to a Web directory, such as Yahoo! or Netscape Netcenter, among others. They provide a subject-tree style catalogue that organizes the Web into major topics, Yahoo! uses 14 categories including arts, business and economy, computers and internet, education, entertainment, government, health, news, recreation, reference, regional, science, social science, and society and culture (Netscape Netcenter has introduced its information under 17 classifications). Under each of these topics is a list of sub-topics, and under each of those is another list, and so on, moving from the more general to the more specific. Therefore, to search an accounting issue, you would select business, after which you would be presented with a number of subtopics from which to choose. Selecting any of these subtopics eventually takes you to Web pages that have been posted precisely for the purpose of giving you the information you need. Yahoo! at *http://*

www.yahoo.com/ has an advantage in that it has a separate section for Canada.

If you are clear about the topic of your query, start with a Web directory rather than a search engine. Directories won't give you as many references as a search engine will, but they are more likely to be on topic. Web directories usually come equipped with their own keyword search engines that allow you to search through their indices for the information you need.

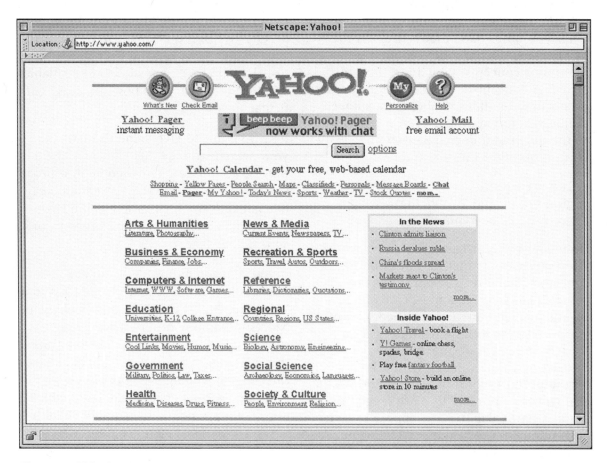

Figure 2.1 Yahoo!

If you're after more narrow, specific information, a Web search engine will be a better choice. More and more search engines are incorporating Web directories into their sites. There are two items to keep in mind when choosing an appropriate engine for your search:

1. use more than one engine, as none is complete in indexing all of the Web pages or usenet groups,

2. the engines differ in how they index the WWW page. Some of the search engines discriminate upper case from lower case; others store all words without reference to whether they are capitalized or not. Some sites index every word on every page while others index only part of the document. For example, Lycos indexes the title, headings, subheadings and the hyperlinks to other sites, along with the first 20 lines of text and the 100 words that occur most often. Another major search engine, Infoseek uses a full-text indexing system, picking up every word in the text except commonly occurring stop words such as "a", "an", "the", "is", "and", "or", and "WWW". Hotbot also ignores stop words. OpenText and AltaVista index all words, even the articles, "a", "an", and "the".

If you understand how search engines organize information and run queries, you can maximize your chances of getting hits on URLs that matter. Initially, set your bookmarks—bookmarking is essential to effective Internet use—to the following two sites: *http://www.search.com/*, maintained by c/net inc., and Net Search, maintained by Netscape Communications Corporation at *http://home.netscape.com/home/internet-search.html*. The former provides over 100 different ways to search the Web using speciality searches, covering a wide variety of business and non-business areas, as well as an "express search" capability that uses the 11 popular search engines. The latter has about 25 well-described links to the most popular engines. Another, even better, site is Virtual Global Search engines at *http://www.dreamscape.com/frankvad/search.global.html*. This Web search site offers the most popular Web search engines, all with easy-to-use forms. Or, if your needs are more specific, you'll likely find what you require there as it has over 1000 fully specialized search engines within 50 categories available to assist you. With these three bookmarked sites, you have the facilities available to successfully navigate the Internet.

Some of the more popular search engines currently in use are:

- **AltaVista.** Located at *http://www.altavista.digital.com/* this fast and massive spider-search engine returns excellent content. It is often regarded as the fastest search engine and the one most likely to return a hit on any issue. Search Web documents or newsgroups by using keywords or phrases. In addition, AltaVista provides a number of specialized services, including locating a person or business, searching in other languages, free email as well as the potential to search under 14 information categories. It also allows searching on the Web or the newsgroups. This engine will display results compact or detailed.

• **Dogpile.** Located at *http://www.dogpile.com* Dogpile provides serious search capabilities. It is a metasearch engine (meaning that it uses more than one search engine simultaneously). It uses 13 search engines to search, among other sources, the WWW, Usenet, FTP and business and other news.

• **excite.** Located at *www.excite.com* it provides a news service as well as search capabilities. You can search for Web documents and classified ads using keywords or concepts. It also searches the past two weeks of Usenet news, and has a site review section (with 50,000 reviews). You enter keywords or words describing a concept.

• **Galaxy.** Located at *http://www.einet.net/* Galaxy has one of the most exhaustive directories of Internet resources. This en-

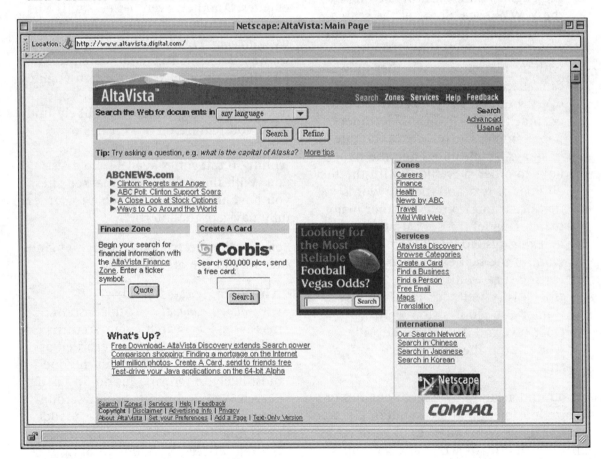

Figure 2.2 *AltaVista*

gine provides three levels of output, from simple links to full descriptions. You can search and browse Web pages, telnet and gopher sites.

- **HotBot.** Located at *http://www.hotbot.com* HotBot is promoted as the number one rated search engine. It exploits parallel computing technology to achieve scale-

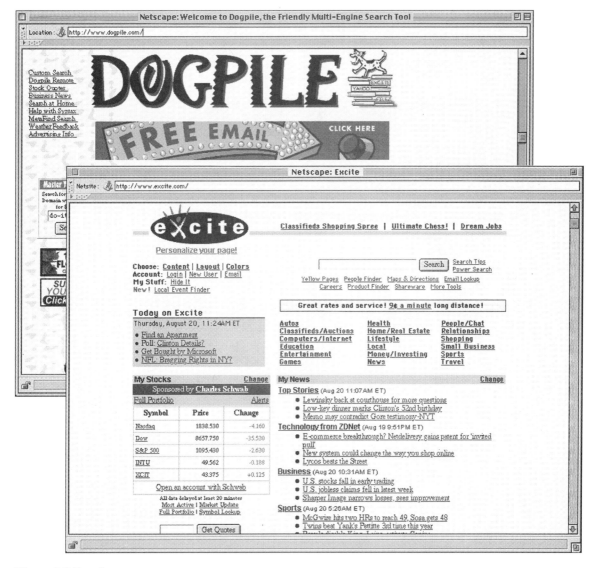

Figure 2.3 *Dogpile*
Figure 2.4 *excite*

able, supercomputer class performance from clusters of reliable, commodity workstations and high-speed networks. HotBot also allows for browsing under nine categories.

• **Infoseek.** Located at *http:// guide.infoseek.com* Infoseek yields highly accurate results to plain English queries. Search and browse Web pages, Usenet newsgroups, FTP, and gopher sites. It

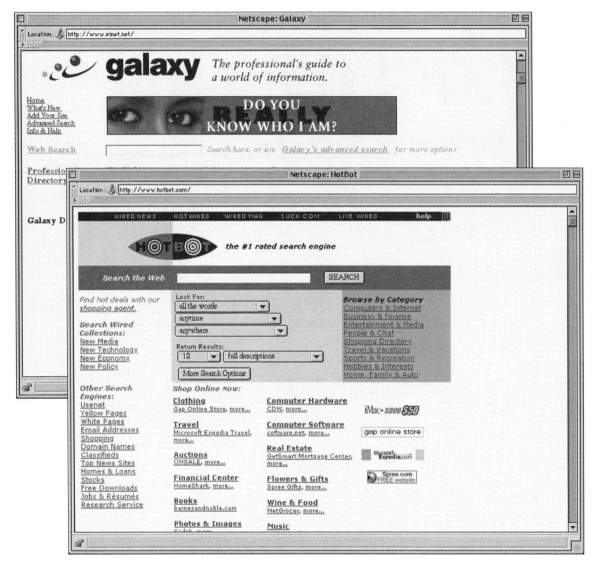

Figure 2.5 *Galaxy*
Figure 2.6 *HotBot*

also provides 18 channels (categories) for searching.

- **Looksmart.** Located at *http://looksmart.com* Looksmart allows the user

to explore through categories using the AltaVista search engine.

- **Lycos.** Located at *http://www.lycos.com* the Lycos database indexes over 90 per-

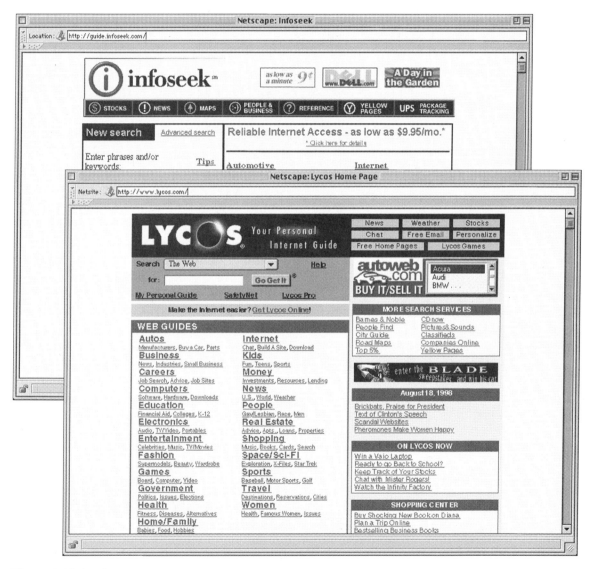

Figure 2.7 *Infoseek*
Figure 2.8 *Lycos*

cent of the Web. *Netguide Magazine* has described Lycos as "The best engine for serious research." It also offers "Lycos SafetyNet" that filters out adult content where such filtering is wanted.

- **Magellan.** Located at *http:// www.mckinley.com* Magellan presents both star ratings and detailed previews of descriptions. Just enter any word or phrase. Its Green Light sites contain no content apparently intended for "mature" audiences.

- **MetaCrawler.** Located at *http:// www.metacrawler.com* MetaCrawler sends your queries to seven different search engines, scores the results into a uniform format and displays them. It searches the WWW and newsgroups as well as other specialized categories.

- **OpenText.** Located at *opentext.com* Canadian-based OpenText provides a sophisticated search engine, offering fast and powerful searches. Every word of every page—millions of Web pages and billions of words—are fully indexed. You can also search under 12 different categories (called slices).

- **SavvySearch.** Located *at http:// guaraldi.cs.colostate.edu:2000* SavvySearch is a metasearch tool. It allows you to enter a query to search up to 24 search engines simultaneously. It searches on up to five databases at once and will search the WWW, email databases, FTP, gopher, and Usenet.

- **WebCrawler.** Located at *http:// www.webcrawler.com* WebCrawler is a popular and fast engine returning relevant hits. It also offers news and other services.

- **Yahoo!** Located at *www.yahoo.com* Yahoo is still one of the better known search sites on the Web today. In addition to keyword searching, it offers a hierarchical subject guide that is well organized and cross-referenced. It also offers news, free email and other services.

DEVELOPING AN EFFECTIVE SEARCH STRATEGY

Most of the search engines that were discussed previously provide facilities for conducting, as well as providing some tips for doing an effective search. Developing an effective search strategy that works in a number of scenarios is not easy. Search engines are trickier than they look. Many can't handle numbers so "SFAS # 7" will usually not work. Also, be careful to avoid common words unless they are linked in an expression. For example, you would not want to use a simple search on "accounting for contingent liabilities". Otherwise, most search engines will return hyperlinks to all Web documents that contain the words "accounting", "contingent", and "liabilities". This will result in numerous URLs, most of which will have no relevance to your search. However, if you enter the words as a phrase, you stand a better chance of getting some good hits.

Most sites offer two different types of searches, "basic" and "refined". In a "basic" search, you enter a keyword without sifting through any pulldown menus of additional options. Depending on the engine, though, "basic" searches can be quite complex. The first rule is to not use too many simple searches. The more information that you can provide as input to the search, the more appropriate the returned information will be. For example, if you do a simple search on "accounting for income taxes" using the AltaVista engine, you will have approximately 1,580,000 hits to go through—*an improbable task.*

Search refining options differ from one search engine to another, but some of the possibilities include the ability to search on more than one word, to give more weight to one search term than you give to another, and to exclude words that might muddy the results. You might also be able to search on proper names, phrases, and words that are found within a certain proximity to other search terms. Some search engines also allow you to specify what form you'd like your results

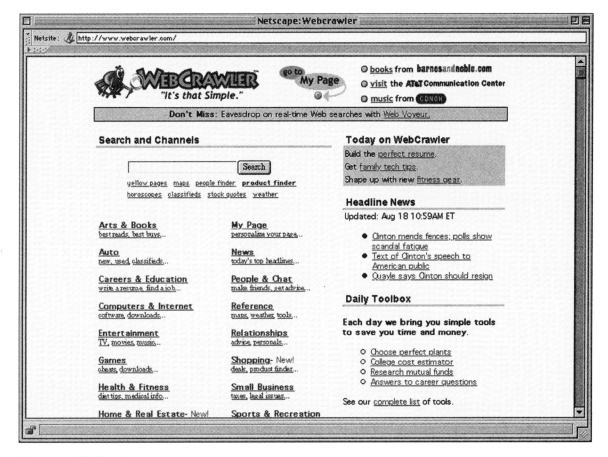

Figure 2.9 WebCrawler

to appear in, and whether you wish to restrict your search to certain fields on the Internet (e.g., Usenet or the Web) or to specific parts of Web documents (e.g., the title or URL).

Many, but not all, search engines, allow you to use so-called Boolean operators to refine your search. These are the logical terms *and*, *or*, *not*, and the so-called proximal locators, *near* and *followed by*. Boolean *and* means that all the terms you specify must appear in the document, e.g., "capital" *and* "assets". You might use this if you wanted to exclude common hits that would be irrelevant to your query. Boolean *or* means that at least one of the terms you specify must appear in the document, e.g., "fixed" *or* "capital". You might use this if you didn't want to rule out too much. Boolean *not* means that at least one of the terms you specify must not appear in the document. You might use this if you anticipated results that would be totally off-base, e.g., if you were looking for Canadian literature, such as "contingent" *and* "liabilities", *not* "fasb".

Some search engines use the characters + and − instead of Boolean operators to include and exclude terms. *Near* means that the terms you enter should be within a certain number of words of each other. *Followed by* means that one term must directly follow the other. *Adj*, for adjacent, serves the same function. A search engine that will allow you to search on phrases uses, essentially, the same method (i.e., determining adjacency of keywords).

The ability to query on phrases is very important in a search engine. Those that allow it usually require that you enclose the phrase in quotation marks, e.g., "accounting for contingent obligations".

If, however, you use the advanced search options, such as Boolean logic (*as*, *and*, *or*, *not*, *near*), date ranges and sorting capabilities, you will get less hits and more relevant information. For example, using the advanced search capabilities on this same search engine, if you do the search "accounting for income taxes" (in quotation marks), you get about 3,700 hits on AltaVista, while "accounting+income+taxes+CICA" (using the Boolean search) you get 292 hits on AltaVista, a much more effective use of your time and resources.

OTHER NAVIGATION AND INFORMATION DEVICES FOR THE WWW

PUSH SERVICES

Rather than having to look for news and similar information, these types of services send information to your desktop directly according to the criteria you set (such as the type of news that you want, etc.).

One of the most popular services is the free PointCast service at *http://www.pointcast.com/button.html*. Headlines move dynamically across the screen, therefore, no surfing is required. PointCast broadcasts national and international news, stock information, industry updates, weather from around the globe, sports scores and more from sources like CNN, CNNfn, *Time*, *People* and *Money* magazines, Reuters, PR Newswire, BusinessWire, Sportsticker and Accuweather, as well as many newspapers. There is also a Canadian edition that provides Canadian news, business information, etc.

OTHER SEARCH TOOLS

Phone Numbers and Addresses

If you are looking for a person or business in Canada, one of the best sites available is Canada 411 at *http://www.newtel.com/communications/canada411.htm*. Other sites can be found by using the search string

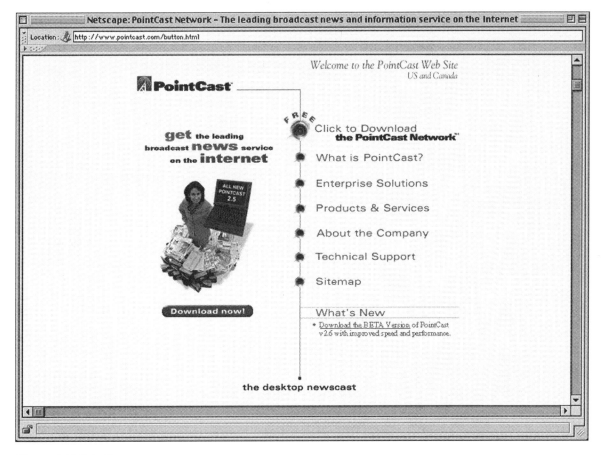

Figure 2.10 *PointCast*

"Canada 411" in AltaVista. This service has indexed most phone books in Canada and is kept up-to-date. Useful sites in the US include Four11 at *http://www.four11.com* and Switchboard at *http://www.switchboard.com*.

There are also a number of active, passive and yellow page sites where you can get information by type of business. Active sites are those companies that deliberately make their identities known on the WWW. The most obvious way is to make

their name part of their Internet address. These include, for example, the Canadian Institute of Chartered Accountants at *http://www.cica.ca* and most major corporations, such as IBM at *http://www.ibm.com* and Microsoft Corporation at *http://www.microsoft.com*. In fact, many corporations are now registering this way in the WWW. As a result, if you are looking for the homepage of a particular entity, first try *"www.thecompanyname.com"*. This may work in a number of cases, saving you the need to use a particular search engine.

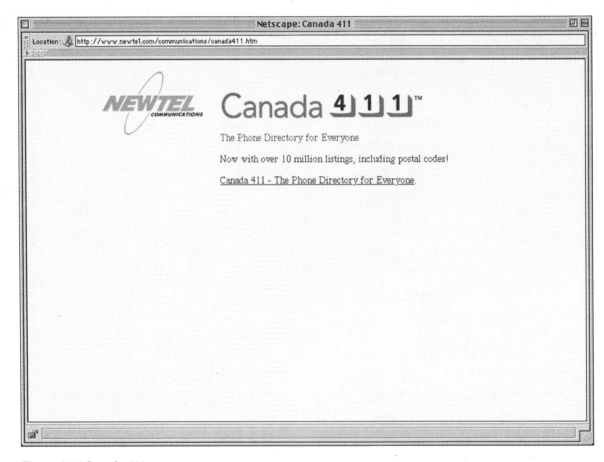

Figure 2.11 Canada 411

Passive sites include those organizations that support or that are against particular businesses. These sites are usually found through search engines or through newsgroup listings.

There are a number of yellow page sites to help you find a business. In Canada, an excellent yellow page directory can be found at CanadaYellowPages.com at *http://www.canadayellowpages.com*. It provides both Canadian and US search capability, as well as links to other yellow page sites. In the US, there are a number of sources, including AT&T Toll Free directory at *http://www.dir800.att.net*, Big Yellow at *http://www.bigyellow.com*, LookupUSA at *http://www.LookupUSA.com* and GTE Superpages at *http://www.superpages.com*. Canadian sites can be located using the search string "yellow pages Canada". The US sites are available by hitting the net search button on Netscape. They are listed as yellow and white pages.

Mapping Information

Some of the more powerful search engines will provide not only an address, but will present it on a map. Lycos and Infoseek are two examples of engines that have road map features that are very exact and very useful. Currently, these are US based only.

Internet Service Providers

If you want to find a list of current Internet service providers, your best bet might be to try The List at *www.thelist.com*, which now lists most Internet service providers.

A Complete List of Registered Canadian Companies

When a Canadian organization wishes to register a domain on the Internet, it can apply to either the CA Domain Registrar in Canada (if it wishes to register in the .ca domain) or the InterNIC (Internet Network Information Centre) in the US (if it wishes to register a descriptive domain such as .com, .edu, .gov, .net, or .org). Some organizations choose to register both a geographical and a descriptive domain.

The list of organizations registered in the .ca domain is updated regularly by John Demco. The list can be retrieved by anonymous FTP, as follows:

Anonymous FTP
   site: *ftp.cdnnet.ca*
Directory: *ca-domain*
File: *index-by-organization*
              (ordered alphabetically)
              index-by-subdomain
              (ordered by subdomain)

The InterNIC does not keep track of US and Canadian registrations separately, so it is impossible to obtain a list of Canadian registrations from the InterNIC. However, the entire InterNIC database is searchable, but only by domain name or organization name. To query the InterNIC database, go to *http://www.rs.internic.net/rs-internic.html*.

SUMMARY OF WEB SITES MENTIONED IN CHAPTER 2

Name/Address

c/net inc
http://www.search.com

Net Search
http://home.netscape.com/home/internet-search.html

Virtual Global Search
http://www.dreamscape.com/frankvad/search.global.html

AltaVista
http://www.altavista.digital.com – soon to be *http://www.altavista.com*

Dogpile
http://www.dogpile.com

excite
www.excite.com

Galaxy
http://www.einet.net

HotBot
http://www.hotbot.com

Infoseek
http://guide.infoseek.com

Looksmart
http://looksmart.com

Lycos
http://www.lycos.com

Magellan
http://www.mckinley.com

MetaCrawler
http://www.metacrawler.com

OpenText
http://www.opentext.com

SavvySearch
http://guaraldi.cs.colostate.edu:2000

WebCrawler
http://www.webcrawler.com

Yahoo!
http://www.yahoo.com

PointCast
http://www.pointcast.com/button.html

Canada 411
http://www.newtel.com/communications/canada411.htm

Four11
http://www.four11.com

Switchboard
http://www.switchboard.com

IBM
http://www.ibm.com

Microsoft Corporation
http://www.microsoft.com

CanadaYellowPages.com
http://www.canadayellowpages.com

AT&T Toll Free directory
http://www.dir800.att.net

Big Yellow
http://www.bigyellow.com

LookupUSA
http://www.LookupUSA

GTE Superpages
http://www.superpages.com

The List
http://www.thelist.com

InterNIC database
http://www.rs.internic.net/rs-internic.html

3 OTHER SECTIONS OF THE NET

INTRODUCTION

Many people, when they think of the Internet, think of the World Wide Web. That particular part of the Internet has become so popular that its name has become almost synonymous with the Internet itself. However, there are other components of the Internet that have considerable potential value to accountants, and are in fact being used frequently, although sometimes unknowingly.

This chapter focuses on those parts of the Internet. The latter part of this chapter also discusses some alternative uses for the Internet. The remainder of this book deals largely with the World Wide Web.

EMAIL AND MAILING LISTS

EMAIL ADDRESSES

One of the most significant uses of Internet is email. Indeed a number of sources believe that email will be the killer application. In the US, in 1996, there were over 40 million users, churning out some 100 million messages a day. This is expected to increase to 170 million users creating some 5 billion messages a day by 2005 (there is no similar data for Canada at this time).

We are assuming that, due to its ease of use, readers are already aware of the programs available for email (such as Eudora, which is Internet specific, and Lotus notes which is used on a microcomputer desktop with a gateway to the Internet).

There can be a problem, however, when trying to find the email address of an Internet user. There is no organization that has taken official responsibility for making Email addresses available for current Internet users. There are a number of organizations that have attempted to fill this void. These include WhoWhere? at *http://www.whowhere.com*, Lycos at *http://www.lycos.com*, and InfoSeek and Internet Address Finder at *http://www.iaf.net*.

MAILING LISTS

These are used in conjunction with email. If you subscribe to mailing lists, electronic mail is sent directly to your email account. The material contained in these groups vary in their usefulness, many involving queries and answers to specific questions posed by a subscriber. There are a number of useful lists for accountants. In Canada, Richard Morochove maintains a list at Can-AccTech. It is currently the accounting technology discussion forum for Canadians. You can also visit AccountNetGuide on the Web at *http://www.morochove.com/netguide*.

In the US and abroad, ANet is a very useful site. Its principal mailing list is ANews-L, which provides information on a variety of forthcoming events, new publications, and important developments on the Internet. You can join these groups by sending an email to *listproc@scu.edu.au* and including in the body of the message *subscribe listname*, where the list name is listed in the following site names (note these are only a subset of the lists that are available):

- **ANews-L.** News. A low-volume but high-quality mailing list that concentrates on news of journals, conferences, seminars, and other matters of interest to the academic accounting community.

- **AAAES-L.** American Accounting Association AI/ES section newsletter.

- **AAccSys-L.** Accounting information systems. The purpose of this list is to discuss all matters concerning accounting information systems theory and practice.

- **AAudit-L.** Auditing. This is a list to discuss all aspects of external and internal audit.

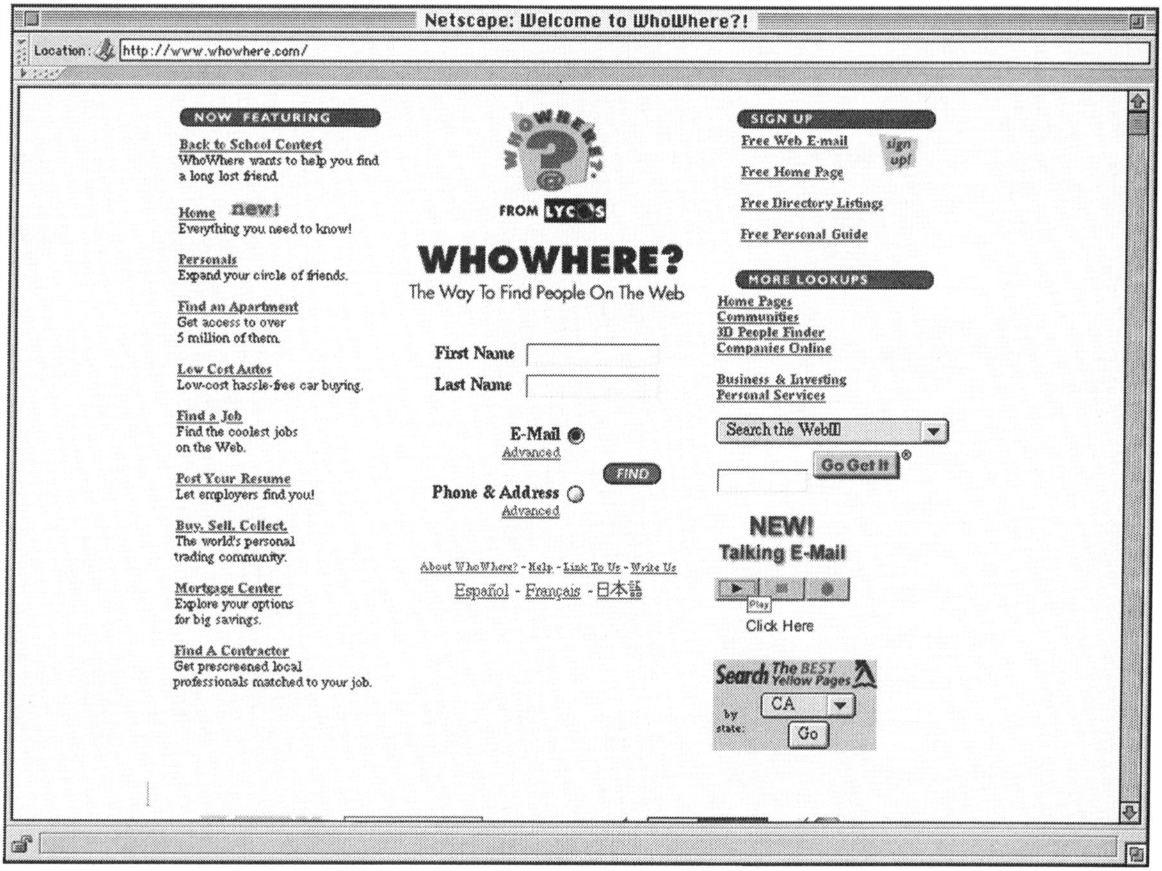

Figure 3.1 WhoWhere?

- **AFinAcc-L.** Financial accounting. This is a list that discusses all aspects of financial accounting.

- **AGvNFP-L.** Governmental and not-for-profit accounting. This is a list concerned with the discussion of accounting for government and not-for-profit organizations.

- **AIntAcc-L.** International accounting. This list discusses all aspects of international accounting.

- **AIntSys-L.** Intelligent and expert systems. This is a mailing list which discusses the application of intelligent and expert systems to accounting and management.

- **AMgtAcc-L.** Management accounting. This is the management accounting list.

- **ASocial-L.** Social accounting. This list discusses all aspects of accounting in its behavioural and sociological context.

For most of these mailing lists, archives of the list are maintained.

How to Get "Free" Email

In the past year, a number of US sites have begun to offer free email, resulting in a significant number of sign-ups (the revenue is derived from site advertisers rather than users). Sign-ups at one site alone are now estimated at over 7,000 per day. Some of the sites that currently offer free email include:

- Juno at *http://www.juno.com* currently has over 5.5 million members,

- Hotmail at *http://www.hotmail.com* currently has over 18 million members,

- excite at *http://www.mailexcite.com* (membership numbers are not disclosed),

- Four11 at *http://www.rocketmail.com* (membership numbers are not disclosed),

- AltaVista at *http://www.altavista.digital.com* (membership numbers are not disclosed),

- Netscape Netcenter at *http://home.netscape.com/escapes/search/ntsrchrnd-A.html* (membership numbers are not disclosed),

- Lycos, at *http://www.lycos.com* (membership numbers are not disclosed), and

- Looksmart at *http://looksmart.com* (membership numbers are not disclosed).

These email services are not provided by Internet service providers (ISPs), rather they are provided by the WWW site.

BITNET Lists

Bitnet is a global network that is separate from the Internet, yet it links academic institutions and research organizations worldwide. Bitnet provides global electronic mail and mailing list capabilities. It is home to some of the more diverse and interesting mailing lists available. Internet users can join any of these mailing lists.

The document "List of all listserv lists known to listserv@listserv.net" (a summary of all Bitnet mailing lists) provides a comprehensive summary of over 4,000 special interest lists. To obtain this listing using email:

Send message to: *listserv@listserv.net*
In text of message, type: *list global*

Viewing the document online through the World Wide Web is particularly useful, since you can quickly browse through the names of various lists or review list types

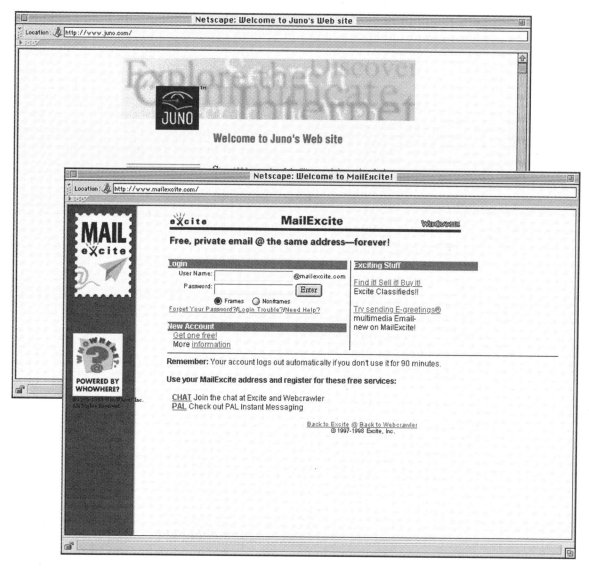

Figure 3.2 *Juno*
Figure 3.3 *MailExcite*

by category: *http://www.neosoft.com/ internet/paml/bysubj.html.*

A comprehensive database of listserv lists from around the world that you can list by category or that you can search for a particular topic is found at *http:// www.tile.net/tile/listserv/.*

USENET – NEWSGROUPS

WHAT IS USENET?

Usenet is described by many as the "world's largest bulletin board system", even though it is definitely not a bulletin board system. Usenet consists of several thousand topic areas (over 15,000 at last count) known as "newsgroups", with a wide variety of topics. Within these newsgroups people discuss, debate, and share information concerning the topic at hand. Given the global nature of the Internet, that anyone can contribute to a newsgroup, and that there are thousands of topics available, there is a wealth of information that you can obtain through Usenet. Some are very useful dealing with professional and business issues, some are just tasteless (most of which are in a non-moderated "alt" section).

Usenet newsgroups are not that different in concept from mailing lists. Since you can obtain Usenet news through most In-

ternet service providers, you can choose to subscribe to the newsgroups that interest you. Given current estimates that some 100 megabytes of information are posted to Usenet each day, you will have to be very selective with respect to which newsgroups you subscribe.

The major differences between Usenet newsgroups and mailing lists are discussed below:

- Email was designed as a point-to-point method of communicating. Usenet, on the other hand, was designed as a mechanism to permit the rebroadcasting of information on a very wide basis.

- Usenet information is more structured, as messages are put into specific newsgroups.

- Most Usenet newsgroups undergo a series of steps of approval before they become widely distributed throughout the Usenet system.

- Usenet news articles have a limited life span. Because of the large number of Usenet messages, many sites will delete messages beyond a certain date.

- Usenet news articles are not sent to personal mailboxes, but are received in batches of postings, which are then made available for reading through newsreader software.

- There are also some "bi-directionally gated newsgroups" within Usenet, allowing automatic distribution to others via a mailing list. This means that if you do not have access to Usenet, you might be able to receive copies of postings to a particular newsgroup through your email account. This feature is not available in email.

In fact, you can use Usenet to get information about mailing lists. A good starting point to get many documents about lists on the Internet is through the Usenet newsgroup news lists. Here, you will find many of the following summaries posted on a regular basis, as well as other information concerning Internet lists.

NEWSREADER SOFTWARE

Newsreader software is the computer program used to access Usenet news. There are no consistent rules in using newsreaders.

- There are many newsreader software packages available.

- Some individuals will use Usenet "on-line", that is, while linked to the computer of their Internet service provider by modem or some other link.

- Some use it "offline", that is, all Usenet articles for groups they belong to are transferred to their computer or local network and are read locally while not linked to another computer.

Millions of people access Usenet news through character-based systems like tin, Emacs and gnus that are found on UNIX. Millions use Microsoft Windows or Macintosh systems (that have a graphical user interface (GUI)) and thus use graphical software like News Xpress (released in 1995) or others such as WinVN 95. The software that you will use depends upon the type of computer you have. If you do not have a GUI-based system Macintosh then you will likely have to access the Internet through a "shell account" and will thus use some type of character-based newsreader such as tin. If you have Windows or a Macintosh, you can use a SLIP or PPP account and can use graphical newsreaders like News Xpress amd WinVN 95 mentioned above.

NEWSGROUP ARCHIVES

Although it is useful to be able to participate on an ongoing basis in some Usenet newsgroups, sometimes you might want to search postings that were made in the past to a particular Usenet newsgroup. Some Usenet newsgroups are automatically archived and are stored on various computers around the Internet. A comprehensive list of archived newsgroups can be found at

- *starbase.neosoft.com/~claird/news.lists/ rootnewsgroup_archives.html*

- *www.pitt.edu/~grouprev/Usenet/Archive-List/newsgroup_archives.html*

The document "Usenet Moderated Archive List" is a good, comprehensive summary of Usenet archives. To obtain this listing using email, send a blank message to *send-mod-archives@ftp.sterling.com*. To obtain this document online, contact *ftp:// ftp.sterling.com/moderators/Archives.html* or *ftp://ftp.sterling.com/moderators/Archives.txt*.

Few Internet service providers are willing to dedicate the hard disk space to archive more than a few weeks of these postings. A few services have arisen that maintain archives for many months or longer, in particular DejaNews at *http://www.dejanews.com* and AltaVista at *http://www.altavista.digital.com*.

SEARCHING USENET

There are also systems emerging that let you search thousands of Usenet newsgroups. For example, DejaNews lets you undertake a search for words or phrases appearing in newsgroups. Other similar services are Infoseek, at *http://www.infoseek.com* and AltaVista at *http://www.altavista.digital.com*.

You should also try Stanford University Netnews at *http://woodstock.stanford.edu* or by email at *info@netnews.stanford.edu*. It allows you to set a search profile of items or topics you wish to track. On a daily basis you are sent, via email, the first few lines of any postings that match your search profile. You can then quickly retrieve the full text of any items by sending back the unique number for that posting. The reference.com site (*www.reference.com*) also lets you establish a clipping service that scours the newsgroup messages each day and sends you an abstract of contributions that match your search requirements.

Even with the above resources, you should be aware of the limitations to searching through the newsgroups:

- Most popular desktop applications do not have the powerful search capabilities of the UNIX newsreaders.

- Many ISPs do not carry all of the newsgroups.

- The ISPs limit the amount of newsgroup entries they will maintain on their systems to two weeks or less because of the sheer volume of entries.

NEWSGROUPS FOR ACCOUNTANTS

Most of the groups appropriate for accounting are included in the biz., news., and comp. categories. In addition, there is a commercial service ClariNews that requires a subscription fee. It redistributes news stories from various global newswires, covering over 300 topics.

FTP

File transfer protocol (FTP) is the oldest (1971), quickest, and cleanest way to copy files between computers on the Internet. If you want to be able to access a huge storehouse of programs, fixes, and updates, find graphics and clip art for your Web and desktop-publishing projects, and most importantly transfer files back and forth between computers, you will want and need FTP. FTP is very appropriate for transferring information between two sites, such as uploading HTML documents for your homepage or transferring documents for mailing and collaboration. In addition, there are files which cannot be accessed through carefully cataloged Web pages. With the enormous library of programs and other files distributed around the Internet, a number of tools were developed to let users find on which computers those files are stored. The services maintain indexes of the files on computers that permit anonymous logins and make finding and retrieving those sites easier.

Unfortunately, FTP is an area of the Internet that requires more basic computer knowledge than almost any other because it requires users to know how to find their way around a computer's directory structure. In an environment such as the Internet, where computers share information so easily, FTP seems ancient and unduly complicated. It requires a knowledge of computers, such as understanding the difference between text and binary files, how to navigate around the file structure of UNIX and DOS computers, and the limitations of filenames in various systems.

For most users of the Web, importing files from other computers is fairly intuitive, as you generally just click on a download button. Often, you will be presented with a list, highlight an item on it, and respond to a dialogue box asking you where to download the file on your own computer. For example, when you go to Netscape to pick up the latest version of its browser, you are using FTP, but are guarded from its complexities. The difficult part is figuring out where the software deposited the file on the user's own machine and then what to do with it.

The relative ease of these uses hides the fact that these transfers are using FTP.

These FTP transfers happen so easily because of the decisions other people have made on your behalf.

As files are incorporated into Web sites, they will be available on searches with the Web search engines. Until then, these older tools may be the only way to find the files you might need. Their utility is expected to diminish to the point where the search engines will be able to provide most of the information you need in the near future. Listed below are some of the more effective FTP programs that could be used in the intervening period.

ARCHIE

Archie is the primary tool for finding FTP files by their title. The Interactive Archie Gateway at *www.bot.astrouw.edu.pl/ archie_servers.html* is a Web-based tool for getting at Archie. Client Archie programs are also available.

WIDE AREA INFORMATION SERVERS

Wide Area Information Servers, or WAIS, at *http://www.wais.com* is an attempt to not only make searching available through the file names, but through the contents of the files, including multimedia and program files. A WAIS engine is available at the WAIS site.

The only way you can get files for your computer from a host is through FTP. If your only goal is to surf around the Web and collect a few graphics, the complexities of FTP are not worth your time. In most cases, this will be the situation that accountants are in. As a result, we have not dealt with this area extensively.

GOPHER

If you are looking for information from the government or an educational institution you may also want to use gopher, in addition to your WWW browser. Gopher is a powerful client/server, menu-driven, retrieval tool. Use gopher to browse through the older and separate gopherspace of the Internet. It should be noted that gopher is the mascot to the University of Minnesota, where the program was developed.

Although gopher has lost favour as the WWW has grown, gopher is still the main tool for getting at the resources of many organizations that have not moved their resources to the Web, in particular, governmental units and large not-for-profit organizations. Much information that has been on the Internet for some time, such as from educational institutions, the government, and not-for-profit organizations, is available through gopher, but is not yet available, or is not available to the same extent, on the Web.

You can bookmark favourite gopher sites to return to them easily. Gopher provides a common interface so that the vagaries of system design do not make finding information on one gopher site more difficult than another.

To find information in the series of menus that makes up gopherspace, you can turn to Veronica and Jughead.

VERONICA

Veronica (Very Easy Rodent-Oriented Net-wide Index to Computerized Archives) is a search tool that searches through the menus in gopherspace and delivers a gopher menu with the results. Because gopher menus not only deliver gopher results, but also FTP, Telnet, Usenet archives, and Web sites, you will find many helpful results in a good search.

JUGHEAD

Jughead (Jonzy's Universal Gopher Hierarchy Excavation And Display) permits more indepth searching through particular gopher sites. The home of Jughead is *gopher.utah.edu.*

In most cases, accountants will not be using gopher; as a result, we have not dealt with it extensively.

INTERNATIONAL RELAY CHAT (IRC)

International Relay Chat (IRC) is a gathering spot for discussions on any topic at any time. It is a real-time conferencing tool where you type messages to a single person or a group. They can respond in real-time as well. Users are identified by screen names of their choice. If you are looking for people interested in chatting in real-time on a topic, IRC is a far more mature technology than the audio groups. IRC software has tools for finding groups by topic, category, and number of users online. IRC channels can offer communication in many different languages.

You find lists of IRC channels at various servers. They are topical, often crude, and often poorly managed. When you connect to an IRC server with your IRC software, you will find hundreds or thousands of channels that are similar to forums, rooms or topics. Most IRC software have tools to make using the list command easier—a command that lets you find active channels with a particular number of participants and where the name of the channel contains a search string. The shareware program mIRC32 lets you filter the groups to find appropriate channels (while reducing the clutter of those you would prefer not to see).

VIDEO CONFERENCING AND ONLINE MEETINGS

The Internet can be used for inexpensive video conferencing or for conducting electronic meetings at low cost. Rather than spending hundreds and thousands of dollars in long distance charges for voice communication only, an Internet user can video conference business associates or others at remote locations with a relatively minor initial cash outlay.

How does one do this? First of all, you need a digital camera that is attached to your computer and focused on you. Two of the common cameras that can be attached to computers are made by Connectix (the QuickCam product line, see *http://www8.zdnet.com/products/content/pcmg/1516/pcmg0171.html*) and Vivitar (such as ViviCam 3000, see *http://www8.zdnet.com/products/content/cshp/1708/cshp0153.html*). You then need conferencing (or meeting) software such as Microsoft's Netmeeting (see *http://www.microsoft.com/netmeeting/*), White Pine's Cuseeme (see *http://www.wpine.com/*), or Netscape's Cool Talk (see *http://home/netscape.com*) to name some that are currently available.

This software allows you to chat through your computer to the other party using voice and video capability. You can perform elementary video conferencing with a designated person having similar equipment. The only current drawback is that refresh rates are not fast and there has to be predetermined meeting times to make sure that both parties are on at the same time.

But this provides many possibilities for accountants and, potentially, their clients. You can use it for working on documents in a group setting, to do a remote presentation, or to contact others with full video interaction, without long distance charges.

For online meetings without video, the Microsoft NetMeeting software can be useful.

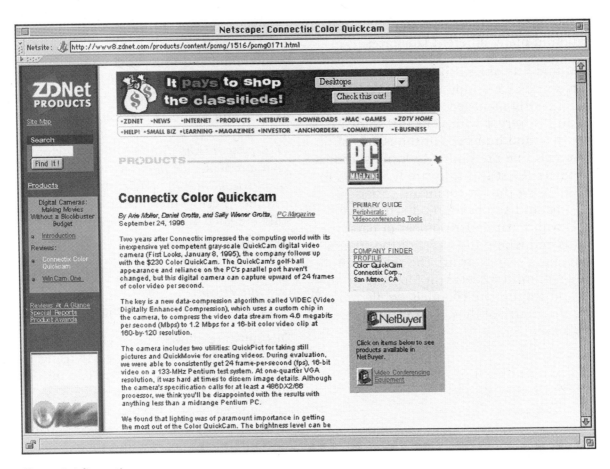

Figure 3.4 Connectix

SUMMARY OF WEB SITES MENTIONED IN CHAPTER 3

Name/Address

WhoWhere?
http://www.whowhere.com

Lycos
http://www.lycos.com

Internet Address Finder
http://www.iaf.net

AccountNetGuide
http://www.morochove.com/netguide

Juno
http://www.juno.com

Hotmail
http://www.hotmail.com

excite
http://www.mailexcite.com

Four11
http://www.rocketmail.com

AltaVista
http://www.altavista.digital.com

Netscape Netcenter
http://home.netscape.com/escapes/search/ntsrchrnd-A.html

Lycos
www.lycos.com

Looksmart
http://looksmart.com

Neosoft
http://www.neosoft.com/internet/paml/bysubj.html

Listserv lists
http://www.tile.net/tile/listserv

List of archived newsgroups
http://starbase.neosoft.com/~claird/news.lists/rootnewsgroup_archives.html and
http://www.pitt.edu/~grouprev/Usenet/Archive-List/newsgroup_archives.html

DejaNews
http://www.dejanews.com

Stanford University Netnews
http://woodstock.stanford.edu

Wide Area Information Servers
http://www.wais.com

Jughead
http://gopher.utah.edu

Microsoft's Netmeeting
http://www.microsoft.com/netmeeting

White Pine's Cuseeme
http://www.wpine.com

Netscape's Cool Talk
http://home/netscape.com

4 ACCOUNTING AND FINANCIAL REPORTING

INTRODUCTION

CANADIAN INSTITUTE OF CHARTERED ACCOUNTANTS

**THE CERTIFIED GENERAL ACCOUNTANTS'
ASSOCIATION OF CANADA**

CMA-CANADA

CANADIAN ACADEMIC ACCOUNTING ASSOCIATION

OTHER MAJOR SITES
SUMMA
RUTGERS
OTHER LINKS

FINDING RELEVANT STANDARDS

INTERNATIONAL LINKS

COMPANY-SPECIFIC FINANCIAL INFORMATION
EDGAR
SEDAR

ACCOUNTING SOFTWARE

SUMMARY OF WEB SITES MENTIONED IN CHAPTER 4

INTRODUCTION

A good starting point for a wide range of accounting coverage on the Internet is found in the Web sites of the professional accounting organizations, like the Canadian Institute of Chartered Accountants at *http://www.cica.ca*, The Certified General Accountants' Association of Canada at *http://www.cga-canada.org*, and the Society of Management Accountants of Canada at *http://www.cma-canada.org/English/cma1.html*. Each of these sites provides information of interest to their members, but more importantly, they provide information of interest to the accounting public.

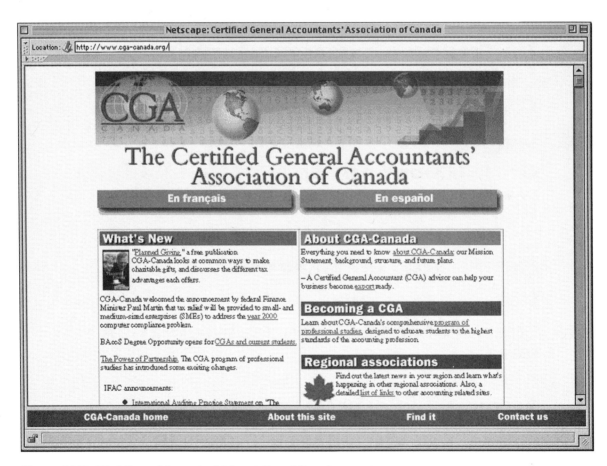

Figure 4.1 *Certified General Accountants' Association of Canada*

CANADIAN INSTITUTE OF CHARTERED ACCOUNTANTS

The CICA site contains pages for each of its departments, including Studies and Standards. Since the standards set by CICA are required to be followed by the *Canada Business Corporations Act*, and other corporate legislation, this covers many people and companies. The site also in-cludes sections on current developments regarding matters outside the standards area. In addition, it includes excerpts from the award winning CICA publication, *CAMagazine*.

As it pertains to accounting, the CICA site places an emphasis on financial reporting, assurance services and criteria of control.

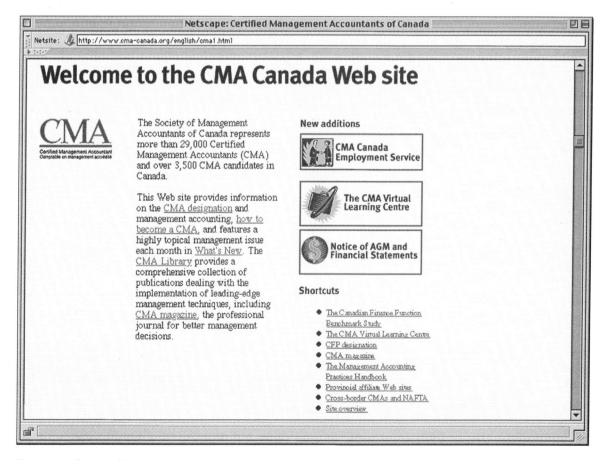

Figure 4.2 Society of Management Accountants of Canada

THE CERTIFIED GENERAL ACCOUNTANTS' ASSOCIATION OF CANADA

Those who are CGAs will be interested in the CGA-Canada site. This site provides information on how to become a CGA, provides links to its regional associations,

provides a private member and student section as well as excerpts from its magazine. It also has education, government, professional affairs and international departments.

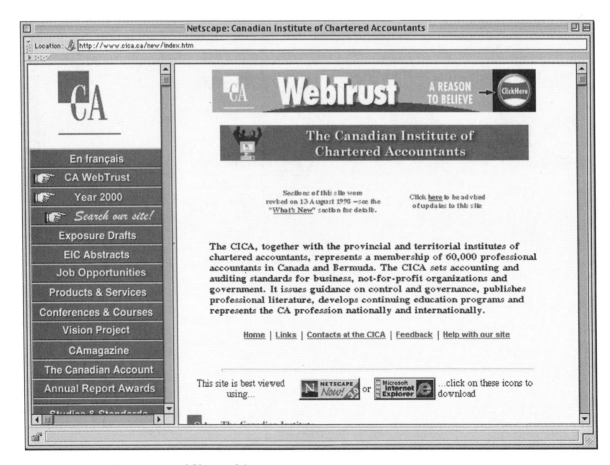

Figure 4.3 *Canadian Institute of Chartered Accountants*

CMA–CANADA

Those with an interest in management accounting would find more items of interest in the site of the Society of Management Accountants of Canada (CMA–Canada). It contains information on the CMA designation and management accounting, how to become a CMA, and features a highly topical management issue each month in a "What's New" section.

The CMA library provides a comprehensive collection of publications dealing with the implementation of leading-edge management techniques, including *CMA Magazine*, the professional journal of CMA-Canada. Publications can be ordered directly from this site, as well as from the CICA site.

CANADIAN ACADEMIC ACCOUNTING ASSOCIATION

This site at *http://www.stmarys.ca/partners/ CAAA/CAAA.html* is the premier association of accountants involved in education in Canada. The site contains a great deal of information useful to academics, such as links to educational Web sites, aids for teaching, comments of exposure drafts of

the CICA and other current and relevant information.

OTHER MAJOR SITES

The various links built into the the sites of the professional organizations can take you directly to the Web pages of other accounting associations like the American Accounting Association at *http:// www.rutgers.edu/Accounting/raw/aaa* and the US Institute of Management Accountants at *http://www.rutgers.edu/Accounting/ raw/ima/ima.htm*. They can also direct you to various accounting journals, to financial markets like the World Bank, Quotecom and the Chicago Mercantile Exchange, to government agencies in Canada and others in the US like the Treasury Department, the GAO and the SEC's EDGAR system at *http://www.sec.gov/edgarhp.htm*. There are also links to the Summa Project that makes up part of the International Accounting Network, collaborated with ANET based at Southern Cross University and Rutgers Accounting Web (Summa and the Rutgers Accounting Web, are discussed below), the Financial Accounting Standards Board (FASB), the universities and several accounting firms.

In summary, the Web pages of the professional accounting organizations include sections on their departments, interest groups, and their magazines (with full copies of selected articles) and publications. Much of the information is useful and applicable to the resolution of practical accounting issues.

SUMMA

The Summa Project at *http://www.summa.org.uk/* is based at Exeter University in the United Kingdom, is funded by the Institute of Chartered Accountants of England and Wales Research Board and provides a Web information server for ac-

counting academics and other professionals. The aim of the project is to support and encourage university accountancy departments and large accountancy firms to provide information on the network, to promote the electronic publication of research and to provide a point of entry to related Web sites of interest. Summa has Web links to most of the international accounting organizations as well as links to FASB and the International Accounting

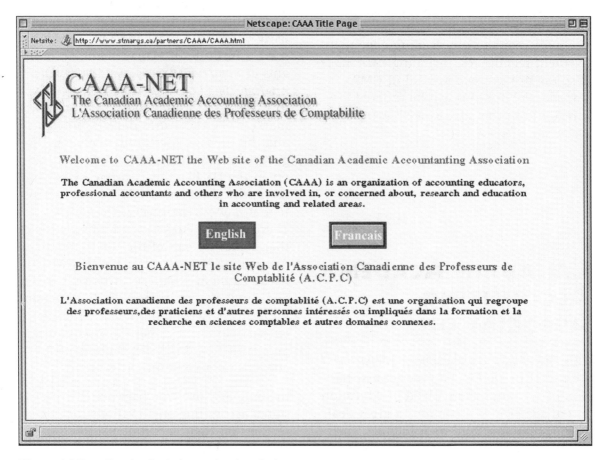

Figure 4.4 Canadian Academic Accounting Association

Standards Committee (IASC) standards. It is an extremely useful site where one can start a search that can lead in many directions.

RUTGERS

For researching an accounting issue, the Rutgers Accounting Web (RAW) site at *http://www.rutgers.edu/Accounting/raw.html* has become a prime reference source.

Figure 4.5 *American Accounting Association*
Figure 4.6 *US Institute of Management Accountants*

RAW is a part of the International Accounting Network, which also includes Exeter University, Southern Cross University, the Swedish School of Economics and Business Administration in Helsinki, Finland, and the University of Hawaii. There is a wide range of accounting topics referred to or discussed in this network, often in some depth.

RAW is an accounting information retrieval system that was established for use

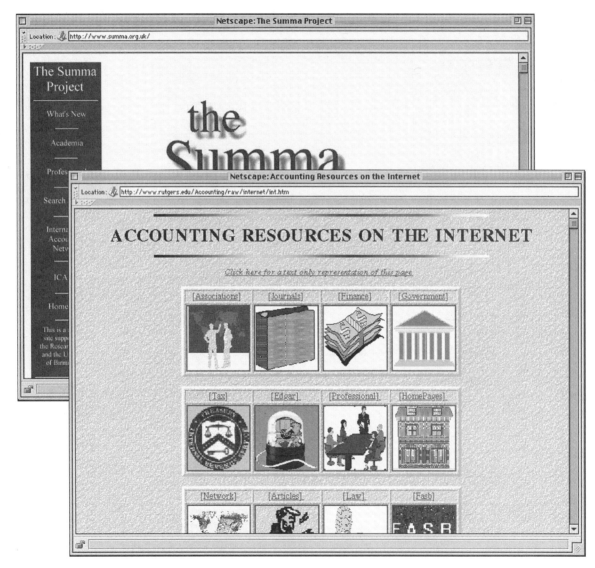

Figure 4.7 *The Summa Project*
Figure 4.8 *Rutgers Accounting Resources on the Internet*

by accounting scholars, practitioners, educators and students. The information is classified according to subject and provider. The educational materials available from this server include lectures, cases, assignments, examinations, course outlines and syllabi. As well, information on specific technical subjects makes RAW particularly useful to accounting practitioners.

In addition, RAW contains one of the top sites for accountants—the Accounting Resources on the Internet at *http:// www.rutgers.edu/Accounting/raw/internet/ int.htm*. It's definitely worth a visit.

OTHER LINKS

These sites provide a wealth of information on the various accounting organizations and their "products". Another useful site for starting a search is the Accountant's Home Page at *http:// www.computercpa.com/* which has a comprehensive list of linked sites related to accounting, finance, government, accounting and educational organizations and other business related sites. It also has a handy list of linked sites for the more commonly used accounting software.

FINDING RELEVANT STANDARDS

Whether researching an accounting issue for academic purposes, or desperately trying to solve a problem for a client, an accountant will usually want to know the standards that apply.

In Canada, the major standard setting body for financial accounting is the CICA, whose site was mentioned above. The Studies and Standards department, which oversees all the standards creation activities, is contained within the CICA Web site on the main sidebar menu. In addition, there is a sidebar for exposure drafts, from which complete copies of the outstanding exposure drafts can be downloaded in Adobe (.pdf) format. Their exposure drafts outline proposed standards on accounting, assurance services and criteria of control matters and are of interest to both practising accountants and those from government and industry who must apply the standards.

Abstracts of the Emerging Issues Committee (EIC) are issued by the CICA and are included in the *CICA Handbook*. Those that have been approved but not yet included in the handbook are available in their entirety from the CICA Web page.

The other major North American standards setting body, which has a high impact on Canadian practice, is the US Financial Accounting Standards Board. It has a Web site at *http://www.rutgers.edu/ Accounting/raw/fasb/* containing numerous FASB documents and information, summaries and the current status of all FASB statements, and complete copies of recent FASB exposure drafts and proposed technical bulletins.

For those who are interested in tracking the activities of FASB in some depth, the site contains announcements of recent board actions and dates and agendas of forthcoming meetings. Moreover, it contains the complete quarterly plan for FASB projects. Finally, the highlights of the site include a comparison of the FASB's international activities to the projects of the IASC.

With the rapid expansion of global commerce, international accounting standards are assuming greater importance. Indeed, many people feel that ultimately all major accounting standards will be set at the international level. At present, the International Accounting Standards Committee (IASC) is the major international standards setting body in the accounting field. It has an excellent Web page at *http://www.iasc.org.uk* and includes many IASC related documents, including lists of standards issued to date and in process, brief summaries of those standards and ordering information. The site also includes recent news of IASC activities and meetings.

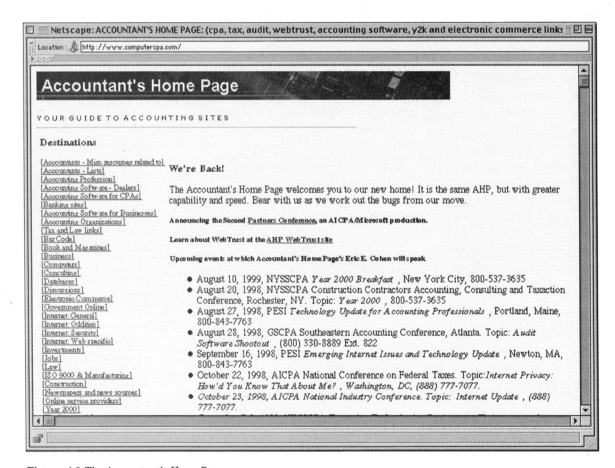

Figure 4.9 The Accountant's Home Page

In the area of management accounting, the major standards setting body is the Society of Management Accountants of Canada, with a Web site, mentioned above, at *http://www.cma-canada.org*. CMA-Canada publishes the *Management Accounting Practices Handbook*, which includes management accounting guidelines, issues papers and other documents. Brief summary information is on the Web site, but full details must be purchased, which can be done from the site.

The International Federation of Accountants (IFAC) has a good page at *http://www.ifac.org* which contains information about its many activities including exposure drafts on management accounting.

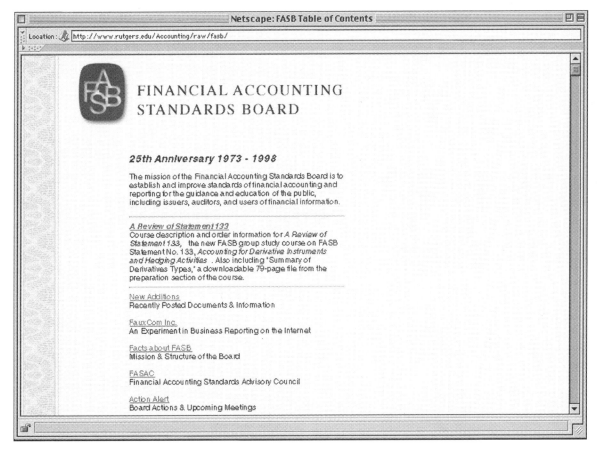

Figure 4.10 *US Financial Accounting Standards Board*

INTERNATIONAL LINKS

Several foreign accounting professional organizations conduct activities of interest to Canadian accountants who carry on business internationally. Some of the more significant ones are The Institute of Chartered Accountants in England and Wales at *http://www.icaew.co.uk/*, the American Institute of Certified Public Accountants at *http://www.aicpa.org*, the European Accounting Association at *http://www.bham.ac.uk/EAA*, and the Confederation of Asian and Pacific Accountants at *http://www.jaring.my/capa*. The latter two contain links to other specific organizations in their geographic areas. The list of links contained in the ICAEW site is particularly good, and has a world-wide focus.

While we're on the subject of links, there are some good sites that devote themselves to providing a full range of links for

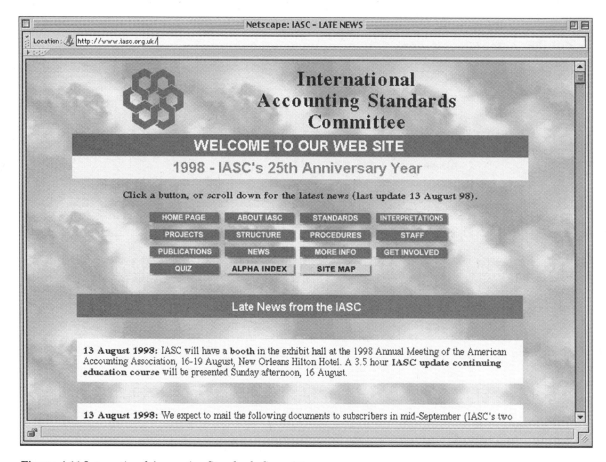

Figure 4.11 International Accounting Standards Committee

accountants. Most notable is Bob Jensen's Bookmarks at *http://www.trinity.edu/ ~rjensen/bookbob.htm*. In addition, there is a good set of links in the site CA-Xchange at *http://www.cax.org*. Although these sites can be somewhat overwhelming, they can sometimes be useful in speeding up a search, provided their index and search facilities are used effectively.

COMPANY-SPECIFIC FINANCIAL INFORMATION

EDGAR

Edgar, the Electronic Data Gathering Analysis and Retrieval service started by the Securities and Exchange Commission in the United States, was the first major attempt to use the Internet as a repository of vast amounts of company specific fi-

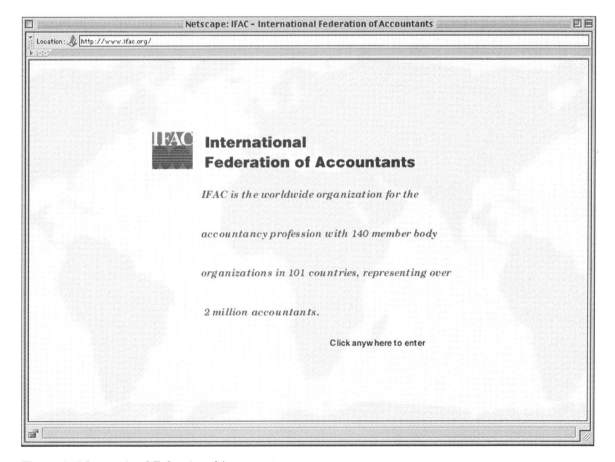

Figure 4.12 International Federation of Accountants

nancial information. The site at *http://www.sec.gov/edgarhp.htm* offers extensive information about the companies that must file with the Securities and Exchange Commission, including complete copies of the forms they have filed.

SEDAR

Sedar, the System for Electronic Document Analysis and Retrieval, at *http://www.sedar.com*, is more or less the Canadian counterpart of Edgar. It was devel-

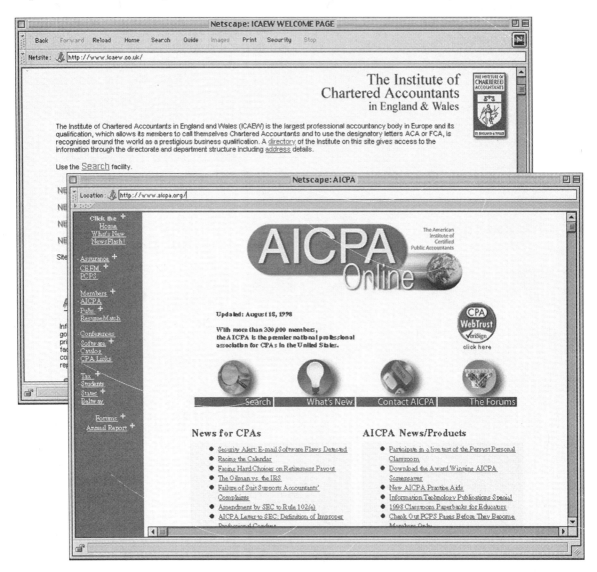

Figure 4.13 *The Institute of Chartered Accountants in England and Wales*
Figure 4.14 *American Institute of Certified Public Accountants*

oped by the Canadian Securities Administrators (CSA), the Canadian Depository for Securities (CDS) and the filing community to provide, as stated in its Web site, three major services:

1. Cost-efficient electronic filing of new issues and all continuous disclosure,

Figure 4.15 European Accounting Association
Figure 4.16 CA-Xchange

2. A corporate database of information on Canada's publicly-listed companies, and

3. Electronic communication with filing partners and with the Canadian Securities Administrators (CSA).

The CSA requires that all publicly-traded companies file electronically. This, in con-

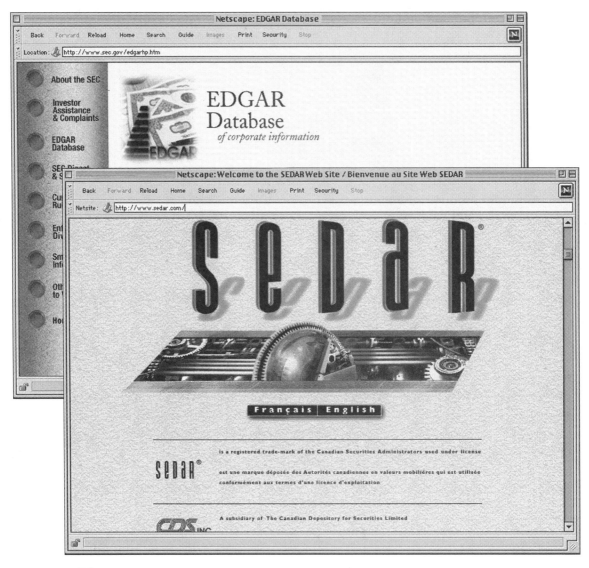

Figure 4.17 *Edgar*
Figure 4.18 *Sedar*

junction with the introduction of Sedar in 1996, will provide a strong incentive for companies to move to electronic reporting of financial information.

Sedar is referred to on the Web site as an innovative electronic link that will enable industry to file all public securities documents and remit filing fees electronically, saving time and money. It will allow users to gain immediate and intelligent access to corporate information in the public domain, and will provide an important communications link among issuers, filers and the commissions.

The site has recently been revised and now includes public filings, a search database, links to regulatory authorities and company profiles as part of its structure. Much has been added in the past 12 months.

ACCOUNTING SOFTWARE

It's hard to keep up with developments in the field of accounting software, but yet, many clients and employers expect accountants to be experts in this fast moving area. One of the best sites for monitoring accounting software is the Accounting Software Page: a subpage of the Accountant's Home Page found at *http://www.computercpa.com*.

Some of the accounting software sites linked to the accounting software page are sites for the lower end systems such as Quicken and Quickbooks at *http://www.intuit.com/* and Daceasy at *http://www.daceasy.com/* sites for the mid-range to high-end systems like Great Plains at *http://www.gps.com/* and Macola at *http://www.macola.com/*, and also sites for the very high-end systems like Peoplesoft at *http://www.peoplesoft.com/index.htm* and SAP at *http://www.sap.com/*.

These software sites tend to hold a large amount of information, some of it quite detailed and certainly very helpful to anyone considering adopting or recommending a new software system.

Following are some of the other more commonly used packages and where they can be found on the Web.

Abacus Accounting Systems is a popular Canadian accounting package available at *http://www.abacus-group.com/*. Abacus Accounting Systems Inc. is the developer of Abacus II, a powerful yet inexpensive accounting solution. Since its release in 1990, Abacus II has established a client base of thousands of businesses worldwide, ranging from small growing businesses to large successful firms in a wide variety of industries.

ACCPAC Plus is promoted as the world's leading software. There are a number of sites that deal with ACCPAC and related products and a number of user group sites. The biggest is ACCPAC Online at *www.accpaconline.com*. ACCPAC Online is an independent site dedicated to the support, education, and advancement of ACCPAC® Plus and ACCPAC for Windows® products and services. It has both English and French forums. It has news, information, technical support, product brochures, downloadable demo disks, ptf patch files, solution providers in your area, advertising, and live world-wide launches for new products.

The ACCPAC site contains news from ACCPAC International about develop-ments and markets relating to ACCPAC for Windows, ACCPAC Plus Accounting, Simply Accounting, and BPI Accounting II. In addition, there are support services, tech notes, education and training information, and tax updates. There are also linked pages to current hot topics such as the Year 2000.

Computer Associates, vendor of ACCPAC, is one of the largest software companies in the world. Their business product sites are

Figure 4.19 *ACCPAC International*

located at *http://www.cai.com/products/bmg.htm*.

Quickbooks, sold by Intuit, is a popular accounting package. That company also sells Quicktax and Quicken. Its Canadian site is *http://www.intuit.com/canada/*. It offers sale and support from this site.

DacEasy provides solutions for small businesses. This site lists DacEasy software, technical tips, online ordering, product literature, and a library of information of special interest to small business. One of its most notable products is DacEasy Accounting & Payroll. It is located at *http://www.daceasy.com/*.

Data Pro Accounting Software, at *http://www.dpro.com/* markets a number of lines of accounting software, including Internet Power Suites. At this site, you can order

software online, find out about products and promotions, and get a guided tour.

Great Plains Software markets its high-end and client/server-based accounting products from this site at *http://www.gps.com/*.

M.Y.O.B. and M.Y.O.B. International, offered by Best!Ware, is a popular entry-level accounting product at *http://www.bestware.com/* and *http://www.myob.com*.

Oracle offers 30 modules for accounting, manufacturing, and distribution at *http://www.oracle.com/products/applications/html/index.html*.

You can find out about Peachtree Software's products and services, including its Peachtree Complete Accounting for Windows at *http://peachtree.com/*.

SUMMARY OF WEB SITES MENTIONED IN CHAPTER 4

Name/Address

Canadian Institute of Chartered Accountants
http://www.cica.ca

The Certified General Accountants Association of Canada
http://www.cga-canada.org

Society of Management Accountants of Canada
http://www.cma-canada.org

Canadian Academic Accountants Association
http://www.stmarys.ca/partners/CAAA/CAAA.html

Institute of Management Accountants (US)
http://www.rutgers.edu/Accounting/raw/ima/ima.htm

American Accounting Association
http://www.rutgers.edu/Accounting/raw/aaa

Edgar
http://www.sec.gov/edgarhp.htm

The Summa Project
http://www.summa.org.uk

Rutgers Accounting Web
http://www.rutgers.edu/Accounting/raw.html

Accounting resources on the internet
http://www.rutgers.edu/Accounting/raw/internet/int.htm

The Accountant's Home Page
http://www.computercpa.com

Financial Accounting Standards Board (US)
http://www.rutgers.edu/Accounting/raw/fasb

International Accounting Standards Committee
http://www.iasc.org.uk

International Federation of Accountants
http://www.ifac.org

Institute of Chartered Accountants in England and Wales
http://www.icaew.co.uk

American Institute Of Certified Public Accountants
http://www.aicpa.org

European Accounting Association (UK)
http://www.bham.ac.uk/eaa

Confederation of Asian and Pacific Accountants
http://www.jaring.my/capa

Bob Jensen's Bookmarks
http://www.trinity.edu/~rjensen/bookbob.htm

The CA-Xchange
http://www.cax.org

Sedar
http://www.sedar.com

ACCPAC
http://www.accpac.com

Quicken and Quickbooks
http://www.intuit.com

Daceasy
http://www.daceasy.com

Great Plains
http://www.gps.com

Macola
http://www.macola.com

Peoplesoft
http://www.peoplesoft.com/index.htm

SAP
http://www.sap.com

Abacus Accounting Systems
http://www.abacus-group.com

ACCPAC Online
http://www. accpaconline.com

Intuit
http://www.intuit.com/canada

Computer Associates
  http://www.cai.com/products/bmg.htm

Data Pro Accounting Software
  http://www.dpro.com

5 ASSURANCE SERVICES

INTRODUCTION

When the Elliott Committee of the AICPA reported in 1996, it set off a new range of potential assurance services that might be offered by professional auditors. The committee's report, the Report of the Special Committee on Assurance Services, is found at the AICPA site at *http://www.aicpa.org* through the sidebar menu access to assurance services. The committee's Web site is their report and presents the services identified, its findings and recommendations, and the other results of their two years of research and deliberations. It is noteworthy that no paper report is to be issued, which sets a new standard for use of the Internet to disseminate a major committee report of this type.

The Canadian counterpart report—The CICA Task Force Report on Assurance Services—sometimes called the Thesburg Report, after its chair, was issued in an interim version by the CICA in May 1997 and in final copy in January 1998. It is included on the CICA Web site at *http://www.cica.ca/new/index.htm*.

Canada and the US have since moved ahead on a joint and cooperative basis, and a joint committee has been struck for that purpose. Accordingly, much more information on this important topic, which promises to revolutionize the auditing/assurance industry, can be expected from both the CICA and the AICPA Web sites, as well as others.

In both the CICA and AICPA sites, interested parties can review the topic from the point of view of their particular function, whether it is public practice, industry, or academia. The information about assurance services can also be explored with regard to new services, customer focus, competitive environment, and information technology. Finally, the AICPA site provides information on the studies and analyses that led to the committee's conclusions.

WEBTRUST

The first assurance product developed by a joint task force of the CICA and AICPA is WebTrust. The CICA and AICPA have broken new ground by offering their members the chance to develop a new business practice: "assuring" that Web sites that offer electronic commerce meet standards of consumer information protection, transaction integrity and sound business practices. This service is based on business to consumer electronic commerce and was designed to help alleviate fears that consumers have in buying product and services over the Internet. The CA/CPA performs a WebTrust engagement following assurance (attestation) engagement standards. If the entity satisfies the three criteria, it will then be allowed to display the WebTrust symbol on its Web site.

The announcement of the service was made in September 1997. The first version of the criteria that is used in the assurance engagement was released in late December 1997 and licensing of members, qualified to perform the service, started in early 1998.

Information on WebTrust, including the criteria, i.e., how to become licensed, and other appropriate information is set out in both the CICA and AICPA sites.

For information on those companies who are currently allowed to display the WebTrust symbol on their sites, one should refer to the Verisign, Inc. site at *http://www.verisign.com/webtrust/siteindex.html* for the WebTrust index. Verisign, Inc. is acting as the certificate authority for the WebTrust program at the present time.

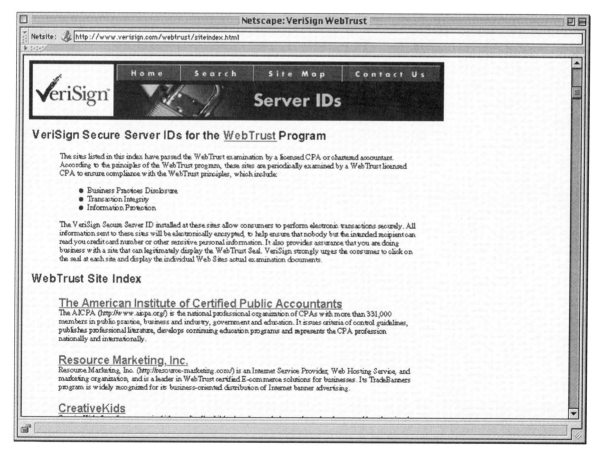

Figure 5.1 *Verisign, Inc.*

EXTERNAL AUDITING

In the meantime, however, the traditional field of external auditing of financial statements continues to be a major industry. The leading North American bodies in this field, the CICA and the AICPA, both have a large quantity of information on auditing in their sites, much of it standards-oriented, since they are the primary standards-setting bodies.

CGA–CANADA

Certified General Accountants are also licensed to practice public accounting in a number of provinces in Canada. Refer to Chapter 4 for a discussion of the CGA–Canada site at *http://www.cga-canada.org*.

CAAA

Another organization of note that has a good Web site covering auditing matters, among other issues, is the Canadian Academic Accounting Association (CAAA) at *http://www.stmarys.ca/partners/caaa/caaa.htm*. The CAAA is the predominant organization of academic accountants in Canada, and the site has a wealth of information of use to academics and practitioners alike.

ISACA

Auditors who focus on business systems have an important role to play in our high-tech, systems-oriented world. ISACA (the Information Systems Audit and Control Association) at *http://www.isaca.org* provides excellent information for systems auditors, as does the Society of Manage-

ment Accountants of Canada at *http://www.visitshows.com/EXHIBIT/mgmtacct.htm*.

INTERNATIONAL SITES

In addition, the International Accounting Network which is a collaboration of three sites—the Acccounting and Auditing Network (ANet) in Australia at *http://www.csu.edu.au/anet*, Rutgers Accounting Web in the US at *http://www.rutgers.edu/Accounting/raw/internet/internet.htm#network*, and the Summa Project in the UK—have expanded their international links to include auditing as well as accounting, finance, regulatory and government. This has made these sites excellent starting points for researching auditing as well as accounting issues.

On a corporate basis, all of the "Big 5" firms have sites in existence as do numerous other accounting firms. There are too many to list, but many of their sites are included in the links provided on sites mentioned in this book, such as the CA-Xchange site discussed earlier. We have also seen accounting discussion groups arise. Once you have subscribed (by email) to these free groups, all email sent to the group is forwarded directly to you. Such groups include Richard Morochove (Morochove & Associates, Inc.) at *http://www.morochove.com/*. Morochove also provides an electronic guide to selected accounting and business sites (with an emphasis on Canadian sites).

Professor Robert Jensen's Bookmarks site at *http://www.trinity.edu/~rjensen/bookbob.htm* contains a wealth of links on auditing as well as the accounting links mentioned earlier and many other areas of interest. For a little comic relief, we have the Home For Neurotically Challenged Accountants at *http://uts.cc.utexas.edu/~gizmo/main.html,* a site that discusses and pokes some fun at some of the accounting pronouncements that exist (although we warn that some readers may find parts of it offensive).

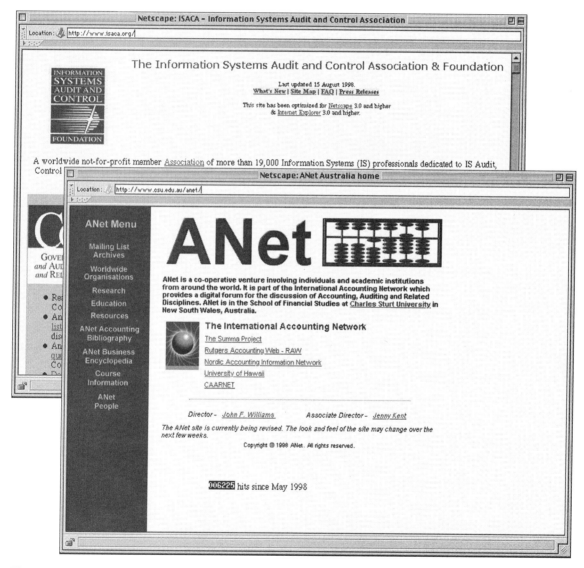

Figure 5.2 Information Systems Audit and Control Association
Figure 5.3 ANet

The International Federation of Accountants (IFAC), as mentioned in Chapter 4, has a good page at *http://www.ifac.org*. One of the more significant activities of the IFAC is the work of the IAPC (International Auditing Practices Committee). The work of this committee is covered in the IFAC Web page, including information on recent standards issued, copies of exposure drafts for download and other related information. Like international accounting standards, international auditing standards are growing in importance.

Of some interest to those who wish to explore the intricacies of external auditing from a particular theoretical perspective, the ABREMA – Activity Based Risk Evaluation Model of Auditing site is of interest at *http://www.efs.mq.edu.au/accg/resources/abrema/index.html*. The model is described as integrating the "three descriptive concepts of audit objectives, financial statement misstatements and audit stages, with the two theoretical concepts of cognitive decision making and audit risk". It is most likely to be of interest to those in acade-

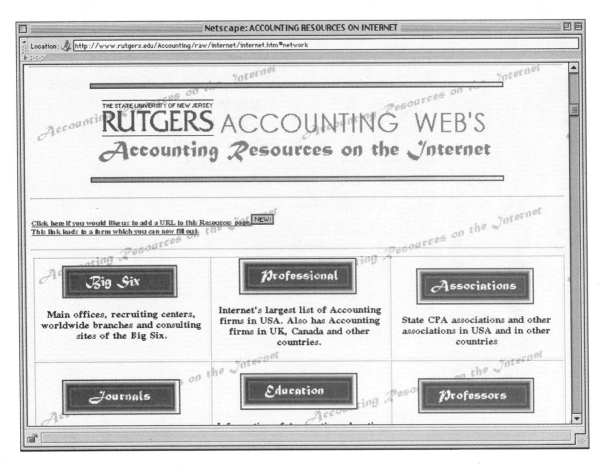

Figure 5.4 Rutgers Accounting Web

mia, practitioners developing their own audit approach, or others interested in gaining a greater understanding of the audit process.

INTERNAL AUDITING

The world of internal auditing is very different than external auditing. In internal auditing, there is a much greater emphasis

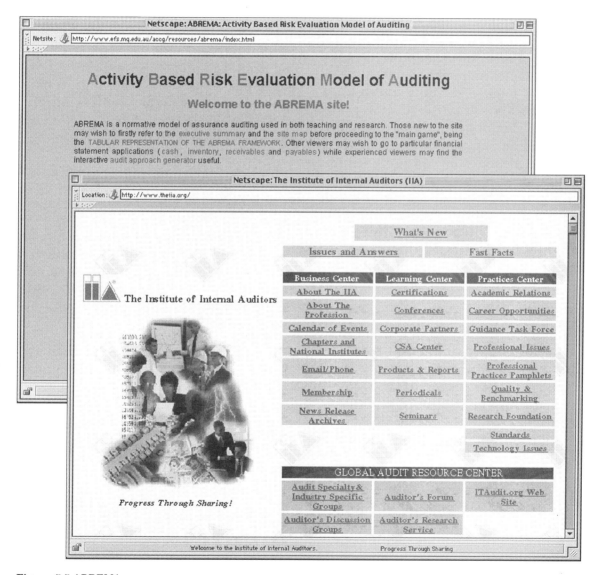

Figure 5.5 *ABREMA*
Figure 5.6 *Institute of Internal Auditors*

on systems and on compliance with corporate policies. But as with external auditing, those who practice internal auditing are organized into a highly competent and widely recognized profession.

INSTITUTE OF INTERNAL AUDITORS (IIA)

The major North American professional organization for internal auditing is the Institute of Internal Auditors, which has a major Web site at *http://www.theiia.org*. Like most of the other professional auditors' organizations, the IIA grants a professional designation—the CIA (Certified Internal Auditor)—and sets standards defining the professional criteria by which the actions of individual members and the operations of internal auditing departments are judged. Members of the IIA are required to comply with IIA standards as a condition of membership and / or certification.

As stated in their Web site, the IIA issues Statements of Internal Auditing Standards (SIASs) which provide authoritative interpretations of the basic standards. SIASs are used to add or change existing General Standards, Specific Standards, and Guidelines. Newly issued SIASs can be found in the Web site, as can exposure drafts of proposed standards.

The Standards contain a code of ethics and a statement of responsibilities. The Code of Ethics outlines the high standards of conduct required of members of the IIA and CIAs. The Statement of Responsibilities provides, in summary form, a general

understanding of the responsibilities of internal auditing.

OTHER GOOD SOURCES ON INTERNAL AUDITING

A comprehensive source of information on internal auditing is AuditNet, at *http://users.aol.com/auditnet*, which was developed as a central electronic resource for the audit community and to provide a global link for auditors. Over time, it has evolved into a significant network of resources available for auditors—the Audit Information Network on the Internet.

Contents include the AuditNet Resource List, which points to a wide variety of sites, an email directory, an Auditbahn (which provides an active vehicle for solving audit problems), a glossary and pages on such timely topics as fraud detection, Year 2000 issues, an interesting set of policies on internet use for auditors and an AuditNet communications network for internal auditors.

A listing of these resources is updated and distributed monthly through the Internet and CompuServe.

PUBLIC SECTOR AUDITING

Another branch of auditing that qualifies as a distinct and significant field is that of public sector auditing. Again, the CICA, through its Public Sector Accounting and Auditing Board (PSAAB) issues pronouncements dealing with standards in this area. As with the other technical pronouncements of the CICA, they are published in a handbook, however, exposure drafts of proposed standards are available from the CICA Web site.

Most public sector auditing is carried out by the auditors general of the federal and provincial governments. The Office of the Auditor General of Canada maintains a site at *http://www.oag-bvg.gc.ca*, where searchable copies of reports issued in recent years can be found.

Most provincial auditors general have their own Web pages, which can be found at the provincial government Web sites mentioned in Chapter 7.

THE DISCIPLINE OF AUDITING

There are many audit tools available on the Web or about which information is available on the Web. Some of these appear on academic sites, and others on commercial sites.

One of the significant aspects of modern auditing is the extent to which technology has entered the field. This includes tools that automate the audit process, as well as those that enable data to be retrieved from computer files being audited.

One useful site is that of CaseWare International at *http://www.caseware.com*. CaseWare is one of the most widely adopted products being used to automate audit workpapers and trial balances. This site has a wealth of information on CaseWare products, including tip of the week, details about recent releases, FAQs on the use of the Caseware products used in practice, a catalogue of tips on application issues, and so on. For those who use CaseWare, or are considering it, the site is a valuable reference source.

AuditMasterPlan is a tool developed by J E Boritz Consultants Limited in conformity with IIA standards for use in developing audit approaches. The site is at *http://www.jebcl.com/amp.htm* and contains a free downloadable demo, online tutorial and various other information about the product, most of which is quite comprehensive.

Audit software that automates the preparation of workpapers or approaches are generally one variety of audit software that is available. Another popular type of audit software is used for data retrieval. One of the most popular of these is known as ACL. The makers of this widely adopted data analysis and reporting tool, ACL Software, has a Web site at *http://www.acl.com*. Although not as comprehensive as the Caseware site, it contains news items and points the way to online support, and various publications relevant to data retrieval and analysis. Another popular audit software is IDEA (Interactive Data, Extraction and Analysis) whose features are similar to ACL. This software is maintained and sold by the CICA. Information on IDEA is available under the "Products and Services" sidebar at the CICA site at *http://www.cica.ca/idea/index.htm*.

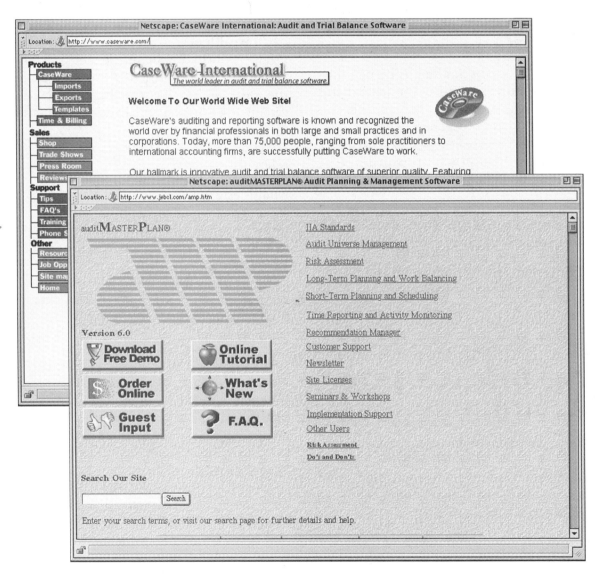

Figure 5.7 *CaseWare International*
Figure 5.8 *auditMasterPlan*

The American Accounting Association—Auditing Section has a Web site at *http://www.indiana.edu/audsec*. Of prime interest to academics teaching or researching au-diting, it also contains useful references and links to related material for anyone interested in auditing as a discipline.

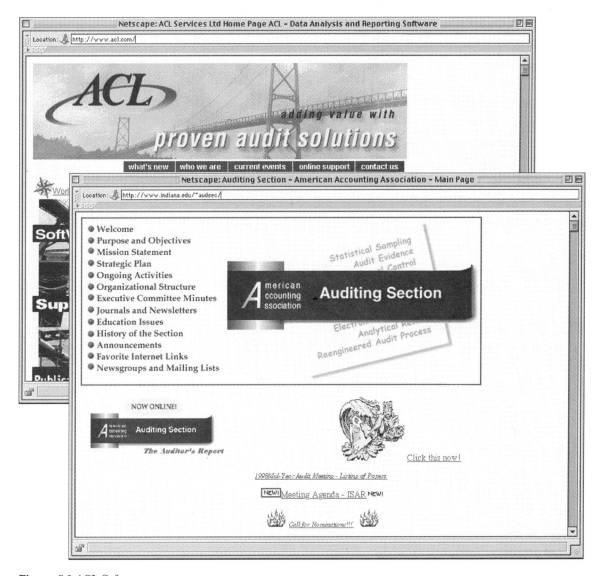

Figure 5.9 ACL Software
Figure 5.10 American Accounting Association—Auditing Section

Summary of Web Sites Mentioned in Chapter 5

Name/Address

AICPA
http://www.aicpa.org

CICA–Thesburg Report
http://www.cica.ca/new/index.htm

Verisign
http://www.verisign.com/webtrust/siteindex.html

CGA Canada
http://www.cga-canada.org

Canadian Academic Accounting Association
http://www.stmarys.ca/partners/caaa/caaa.htm

Information Systems Audit and Control Association
http://www.isaca.org

Society of Management Accountants of Canada
http://www.visitshows.com/EXHIBIT/mgmtacct.html

Accounting and Auditing Network (ANet)
http://www.csa.edu/anet

Rutgers Accounting Web
http://www.rutgers.edu/Accounting/raw/internet/internet.htm#network

CA-Xchange
http://www.cax.org

Morochove & Associates, Inc.
http://www.morochove.com

Professor Robert Jensen's Bookmarks
http://www.trinity.edu/~rjensen/bookbob.htm

Home For Neurotically Challenged Accountants
uts.cc.utexas.edu/gizmo/main.html

International Federation of Accountants
http://www.ifac.org

ABREMA
http://www.efs.mq.edu.au/accg/resources/abrema/index.html

The Institute of Internal Auditors
http://www.theiia.org

AuditNet Homepage
users.aol.com/auditnet

Office of the Auditor General of Canada
http://www.oag-bvg.gc.ca

Auditserve Inc.
http://www.auditserve.com/index.html

Caseware International
http://www.caseware.com

AuditMasterPlan
http://www.jebcl.com/amp.htm

ACL
http://www.acl.com

IDEA
http://www.cica.ca/idea/index.htm

The American Accounting Association—Auditing Section
http://www.indiana.edu/~audsec

6 FINANCE AND THE WEB

INTRODUCTION

The Web is an excellent information source for finance and related information for the accountant. This chapter discusses valuable sites for getting information on financial institutions and related services in Canada, and to a lesser extent, abroad. It also includes information on sites where you can do your banking, a major development over the past couple of years.

SPECIFIC INFORMATION VS GENERAL FINANCE THEORY

Although specific URLs are provided in this chapter, there are three very good general sites that have significant links. The most comprehensive site is the Canadian Financial Network Inc. at *http://www.canadianfinance.com/cfnbase/cdnbase.htm*. Another good Canadian-based link site is Financial Information Link Library at *http://www.mbnet.mb.ca/~russell*. Finally, a comprehensive site that provides information about sites in Canada and around the world is Finance Net at *http://www.finance-net.com*.

This chapter concentrates on those sites that relate to organizations and financial

institutions, and we offer a good summary of the content. To utilize the Web for the purpose of finding information about specific financial concepts, it is in many cases most practical to use the various search engines to find a specific term (such as "cost+of+capital" or "EOQ" or "economic order quantity").

For example, using "cost+of+capital" in an AltaVista search results in over 3200 hits that discuss what it is, how it is calculated, and other related areas. As always, it is important to formulate queries carefully. For example, a search using the acronym EOQ results in 2000 hits, many of which are not relevant (they relate to the European Quality Awards, among others). As a result, the term "economic order quantity" (with quotes) should be used.

It should be noted that this chapter will not be addressing common shares; they are discussed in Chapter 12, Securities Information. Rather, this chapter will discuss bank sites, other debt issuing/investment sites, and other places to obtain finance information.

This chapter is organized under the following headings:

- financial news – to assist the accountant with general business and finance information that can be retrieved online,

- investment research – that the accountant or the client can use. This is not restricted to any specific financial institution,

- banks, trust companies and credit unions – a reasonably comprehensive list of financial institutions that are available online,

- finance centres with investor information,

- mutual funds and financial planning, and

- finance software and utilities.

FINANCIAL NEWS

There are, of course, a number of publications that provide finance news, in fact, it is a part of most newspapers in Canada and abroad. The sites listed below represent a segment of those that concentrate on business and finance news.

To start with, Canada's two leading financial newspapers, *The Financial Post* and *The Globe and Mail*, have sites at *http://www.canoe.com/FP/home.html* and *http://www.globeandmail.ca* respectively. These sites contain extensive up-to-date information about financial and other business related events. For those willing to pay a fee, Info Globe at *http://qsilver.queensu.ca/*

Figure 6.1 CFN

law/infoglob.htm provides very extensive access to the databases of *The Globe and Mail* and other Thomson newspapers.

To give equal time, access to Southam newspapers can be found at Southam, Inc at *http://www.southam.com*. It provides full text of cover stories and lead articles in current and back issues and has a searchable database providing brief profiles and contact information.

Another large database is found at Infomart at *http://www.infomart.ca*. It provides

access to the products and services of both Infomart Online and DIALOG. There are over 2000 databases containing over 500 million articles, abstracts and citations covering a variety of topics, with particular emphasis on news, business, science and technology.

If you wish to go back to a more primary source, Canada NewsWire Ltd at *http://www.newswire.ca* provides a daily list of news releases, a searchable database for past news releases, and corporate reports.

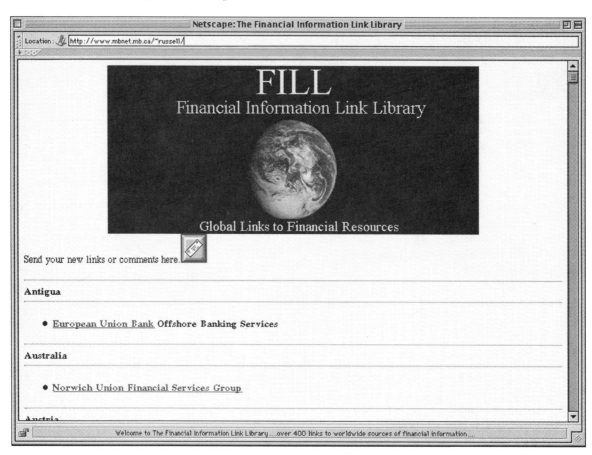

Figure 6.2 *Financial Information Link Library*

To find copies of Canadian press releases, try consulting Canadian Corporate News at *http://www.cdn-news.com*. They tout themselves as the place to find press releases before other sources carry them.

INVESTMENT RESEARCH

There are a number of sites that provide online investment research for finance activities. Most are free, some provide lim-

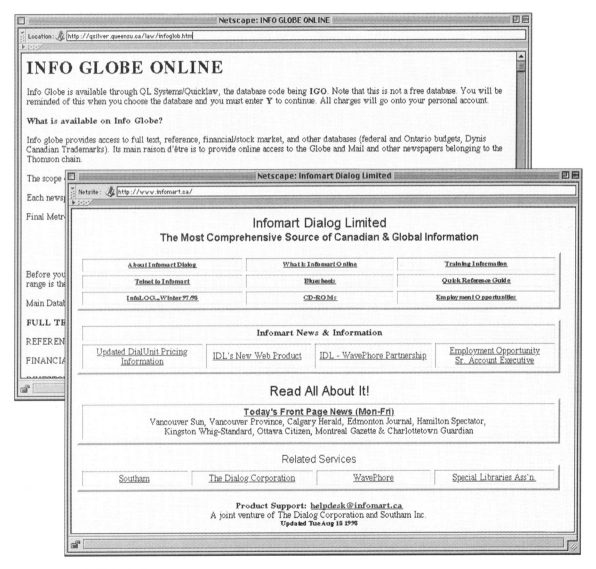

Figure 6.3 *Info Globe Online*
Figure 6.4 *Infomart*

ited non-membership access and others are membership driven. Following are some selected sites.

The Canadian Society of Technical Analysis at *http://www.csta.org* features, among other things, a code of ethics, library resources, and CSTA school newsletter. This site is a good start for investigating investment research, as it provides a good range of information and offers avenues for searching out other sites.

The Toronto Society of Financial Analysts has a site at at *http://www.aimr.org/aimr/societies/local/toronto.html*. It is a member of AIMR, the Association for Investment Management and Research (AIMR), an international, non-profit organization of investment practitioners and educators headquartered in Charlottesville, Virginia. AIMR has a Web site at *http://www.aimr.org*.

Figure 6.5 Canadian Corporate News

Finally, a major source of comprehensive information for investment research is Standard & Poor's Compustat at *http://www.compustat.com*. This site is almost a standard in the industry.

Specific corporate information can be found at various sites, including Canadian Industry Overviews, at *http://strategis.ic.gc.ca/sc_ecnmy/sio/homepage.html*. This site provides statistical and qualitative information on over 200 Canadian manufacturing industries with special emphasis on production, international trade, and detailed sector level performance. The reports are prepared by the Canadian federal government.

Canadian Investor Relations and Corporate Communications at *http://www.fin-info.com*, provides an index to any Canadian public company or bond issuing Crown corporation on the TSE, ASE, VSE and MSE. Stock quotes, stock graphs and news releases are available for listed companies.

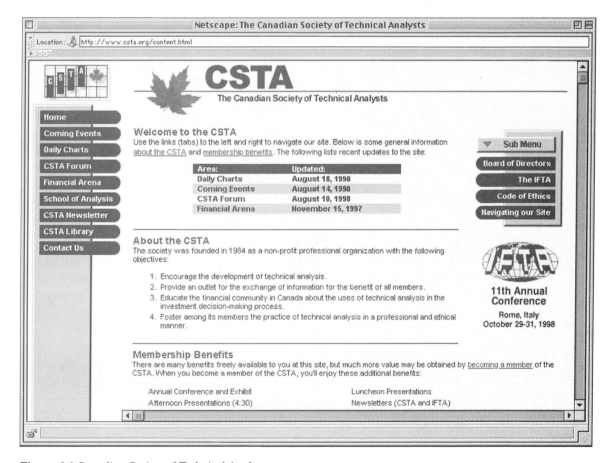

Figure 6.6 *Canadian Society of Technical Analysts*

Another "must" site for Canadian investors is Micromedia Ltd. at *http://www.mmltd.com/files/homepage.html*. It provides a searchable database of corporate filings (from 1985), database indexes, and the current issue of the OSC (Ontario Securities Commission) Bulletin.

For the oil industry, in-depth information can be found at the site of the Canadian Oil and Gas Financial Data Base at *http://www.mossr.com*. It provides closing stock prices for a number of Canadian oil and gas companies and also some natural gas export statistics, volumes and prices. Similar information for the mining industry can be found at Robertson Info-Data Inc. at *http://www.info-mine.com*. It provides current and archived mining news and has a searchable database of contact information of mining.

Finally, stock quotes can be found at many sites. One of them is Stock-Watch.com at *http://www.canada-stockwatch.com* which provides real time quotes with full market portfolio, news and statistics. This site contains almost 500,000 news releases. Another notable source of quotes is StockHouse at *http://www.stockhouse.com*. This is an Online Journal covering micro and small capital stocks in Canada and the US.

BANKS AND CREDIT UNIONS

There are a number of Canadian banks and credit unions that have sites on the Web. Most provide information as to the services they perform, as well as contact data. As mentioned earlier, most now feature online banking for their customers and some have online loan application features. Since the list is ever growing, we cannot purport to be addressing all of them. The ones that we have noted here are listed in alphabetical order, with the banks listed first.

The Web site of the Canadian Bankers Association (CBA) at *http://www.cba.ca/eng/index.htm* warrants a special mention as it features a good deal of information about Canadian banking and also provides links to all the Canadian chartered banks. The CBA is a professional industry association that provides information, research, advocacy, education and operational support services primarily to its members, the chartered banks of Canada.

All the big banks, of course, have major Web sites as outlined below:

Bank of Montreal at *http://www.bmo.com* and the Royal Bank of Canada at *http://www.royalbank.com* are two of Canada's largest banks and of course may end up being Canada's largest bank.

The Web sites for the Toronto Dominion Bank at *http://www.tdbank.ca/tdbank*, Scotiabank at *http://www.scotiabank.ca*, and the Canadian Imperial Bank of Commerce at *http://www.cibc.com* are extremely comprehensive and contain essentially similar but very useful information on all aspects of banking and the other products they offer, such as mutual funds, investment products, etc.

Various other banks have Web sites and their URLs can be found on the CBA site.

Examples are the Laurentian Bank of Canada at *http://www.laurentianbank.com* and the Banca Commerciale Italiana of Canada (BCI Bank) at *http://www.bcibank.ca*.

Finally, a bank of considerable interest to many accountants and their clients is the Business Development Bank of Canada at *http://www.bdc.ca/bdc/home/index.html*. The BDBC is touted as Canada's "small business" bank, and places a particular focus on the emerging and exporting sectors of the economy.

With the discussion about the possible impact of the proposed bank mergers on Canadian banking customers, some attention has turned to credit unions as a possible answer to perceptions that the big banks might be impersonal. There are a great many credit unions in Canada, many of which have Web sites.

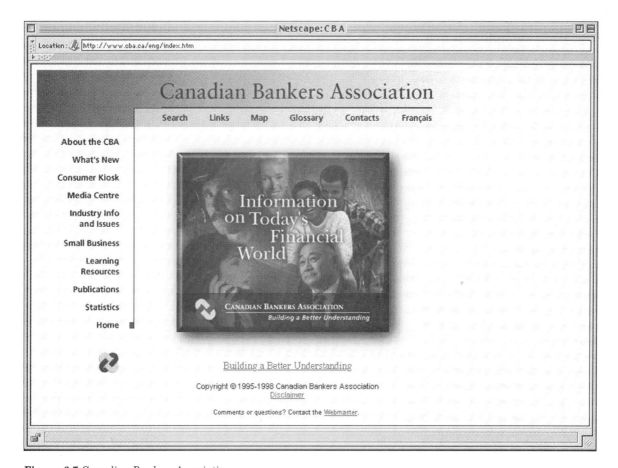

Figure 6.7 Canadian Bankers Association

There are several sites that offer links to, or information about, specific credit unions. The best is the site of Credit Union Central of Canada at *http://www.cucentral.ca/home.html*. This Web site explains how the credit union system is structured, from local credit unions composed of shareholder members, to the provincial and national tiers designed to support local credit unions in providing state-of-the-art financial services that offer distinctive advantages to members. The site provides links to the provincial credit union sites at *http://www.cucentral.ca/ provcuc/index.html*. The provincial sites, in turn, provide links to specific credit union Web sites. This is the best way to search down credit union Web sites.

Some of the sites we reviewed are listed below:

Credit Union Atlantic at *http:// www.cua.com* serves the Atlantic region. Credit Union Central Ontario at *http:// www.cuco.on.ca* is the only organization in Ontario that provides a full range of oper-

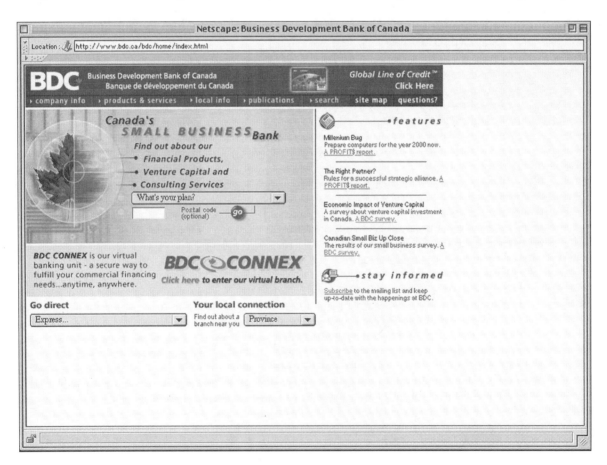

Figure 6.8 *Business Development Bank of Canada*

ational and financial services dedicated to credit unions. Credit Unions of Saskatchewan at *http://www.saskcu.com* identifies over 300 credit union locations across Saskatchewan. Manitoba's Credit Unions at *http://www.creditunion.mb.ca* provides general and location information for credit unions in Manitoba.

One of Canada's largest credit unions is the Surrey Metro Savings Credit Union at *http://www.metrosavings.com*. It is Canada's second largest credit union serving over

125,000 customers in and around Surrey, B.C.

Some of the other credit unions are the Latvian Credit Union Ltd. at *http://www.lcu.homesite.ca*, the Mt. Lehman Credit Union at *http://www.mtlehman.com*, the Toronto Electrical Utilities Credit Union at *http://www.teucu.com*, which has a membership of over 2300, the Assiniboia Credit Union at *http://www.cypronet.com/~acu/info.html*, and Bergengren Credit Union at *http://www.bergengrencu.com* in Anti-

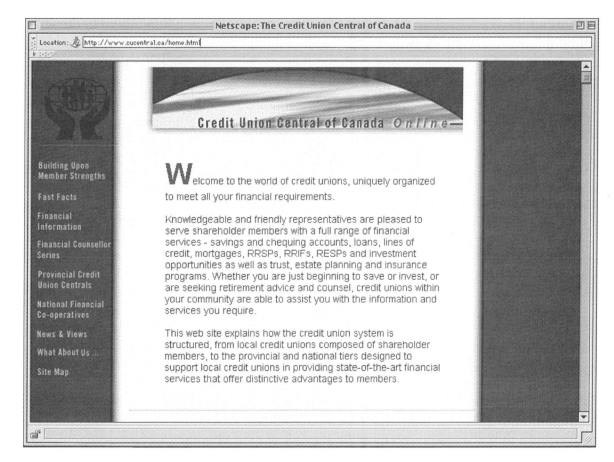

Figure 6.9 Credit Union Central of Canada

gonish, Nova Scotia, which has 12000 members and over $70 million in assets.

FINANCE CENTRES WITH INVESTMENT INFORMATION

Another significant part of finance is the provision of management and related financial information. The following sites follow discuss which organizations in Canada, involved in that activity, have Web sites. Again, the site listing is not meant to be all-inclusive.

- Altamira at *http://www.altamira.com* provides news services, a resource centre to review market commentary, financial planning articles, financial planning tools, such as an RRSP calculator, a discussion forum and an online office.

- Fidelity Mutual Funds at *http://www.fid-inv.com* provides market news, data and commentary and investment planning information and tools.

- Wood Gundy PCI at *http://www.woodgundypci.com/home/index.html* provides information about their broad range of services in a wide spectrum of credit and capital market capabilities.

- Investment Brokerages Guide at *http://www.cs.cmu.edu/~jdg/invest_brokers* provides the individual investor with an overview of the brokerage industry. It compares the available services and commission rates of over a hundred brokerages across the world. Also, it provides contact information for brokerages, including links to their homepages, when available.

- MC&A Net Broker at *http://www.netaxis.qc.ca/cma* features NetBroker, bonds and equity research, and online forms. It is noteworthy that most of the bank sites mentioned above also provide discount brokers' services through their Web sites.

The major investment brokers have Web sites, including Midland Walwyn at *http://www.midwal.ca*, Nesbitt Burns at *http://www.bmo.com*, possibly Canada's largest full-service investment firm, and RBC Dominion Securities Inc. at *http://www.rbcds.com*. The latter features private client services, investment banking, global markets, careers, a site map, and links to the Royal Bank of Canada.

Finally, Scotia Capital Markets at *http://www.scotiacapital.com* features private client information, morning news and updates, instant information, an office locator and other material.

MUTUAL FUNDS AND FINANCIAL PLANNING

Mutual funds continue to be one of the most popular methods of investing by Canadians. There is a wealth of information on the Net about these investment vehicles. Similar to our prior discussions, we have attempted to provide a good cross section of mutual funds and financial planners that have an Internet presence. Again the list is not all-inclusive. We begin with some of the general or overview sites, many of which contain links to specific mutual funds.

Advice as to mutual fund investing is an important function of financial planners. The Canadian Institute of Financial Planning at *http://www.mutfunds.com/cifp* is one of the major Canadian associations in this field. It offers the Certified Financial Planner Program, a series of six correspondence courses which, when completed successfully, satisfy the education requirement for the "Certified Financial Planner".

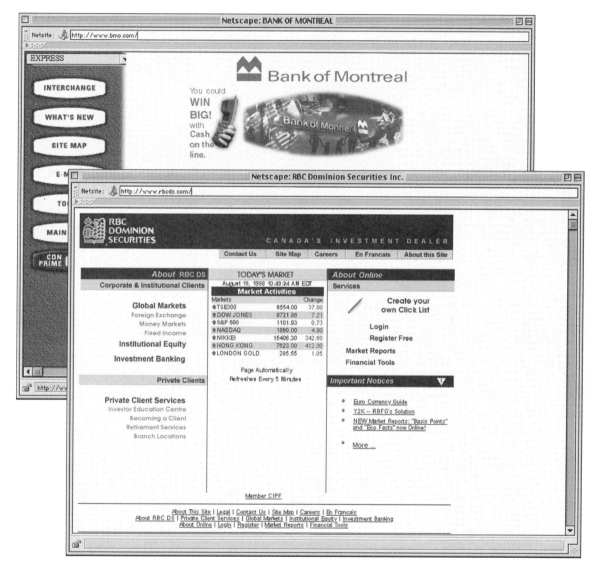

Figure 6.10 *Nesbitt Burns*
Figure 6.11 *RBC Dominion Securities Inc.*

The Canadian Association of Financial Planning at *http://www.cafp.org* contains information for consumers and for planners about mutual fund investing, among other things. The Canadian Financial Advisory Service at *http://cfas.com* provides information on various financial planning options and support services.

Assistance in selecting a financial planner is available on the Web at a site called Selecting a Financial Planner, offered by the

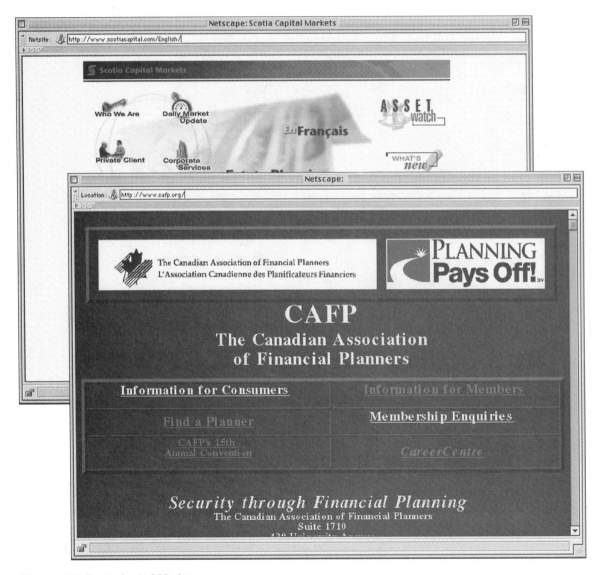

Figure 6.12 *Scotia Capital Markets*
Figure 6.13 *Canadian Association of Financial Planners*

Better Business Bureau, and located at *http://www.bbb.org*. The site provides instant access to business and consumer alerts as well as helpful resources. It also allows consumers to file a complaint online.

The Canadian Mutual Fund Library at *http://www.fundlib.com* is designed to educate and inform investors about Canadian mutual funds and has a wealth of information on the topic.

The Financial Service Network at *http://www.fsn.ca/cgi-bin/DisplayPage?fsn@5.0* is part of a larger site containing general investment information. Fundata Canada Inc. at *http://www.fundata.com* provides significant performance and other data for Canadian mutual funds.

Of course, all of the big banks offer mutual funds and their sites contain information about those funds, and the specific fund products they offer. For example, First Canadian Mutual Funds (Bank of Montreal) at *http://www.fcfunds.bomil.ca* provides online investment information and research, providing data and tools for investors. Royal Mutual Funds at *http://www.royalbank.com/english/rmf* features fund and performance information models and reports among its extensive information data base. TD Bank's Mutual Fund Centre at *http://www.tdbank.ca/mutualfund* is part of the TD Bank, as previously mentioned.

The Investment Funds Institute of Canada at *http://www.mutfunds.com/ific* features, among other data, what's new,

publications, member services and mutual fund links.

Investment Challenge at *http://inv-chal.yorku.ca* is a leading provider of stock market simulations throughout North America. The simulations provide a realistic forum to test investment strategies and learn about the markets.

If you are one of those baby boomers looking at retirement, then RetireWeb at *http://www.retireweb.com* may be of interest to you. This is a site packed with financial planning information for Canadians of all ages to help them with all stages of retirement, saving for retirement, options at retirement, and post retirement.

Some of the specific mutual find and mutual fund manager sites that we looked at are listed below:

• Affinity Group Inc. at *http://www.affinitygrp.com* represents five of Canada's leading mutual fund managers who were chosen on the basis of their performance, reputation, experience, size and consistency. These include AGF Management Ltd., C.I. Mutual Funds, Mackenzie Financial Services Inc., Templeton Management Ltd., and Trimark Investment Management Inc.

• AGF Group of Funds at *http://www.agf.com* provides information as to performance and market and provides an investment calculator and an enquiry service. It is one of Canada's largest mutual fund managers.

• Altamira Investment Services Inc. at *http://www.altamira.com* has managed corporate, pension and private investments for over 25 years. The site features discussions, information about mutual funds, and other relevant data and information.

- Dynamic Mutual Funds at *http://www.dynamic.ca* features NAV, fund descriptions, outlook, understanding mutual funds, etc.

- Fidelity Mutual Funds at *http://www.fid-inv.com* features, among other

things, market news, data and commentary, investment planning information and tools, and performance and investing information for fidelity & nonfidelity funds.

- Investors Group at *http://www.investorsgroup.com* is one of Canada's largest mutual fund groups.

- Leeland Financial Group at *http://www.cadvision.com/Home_Pages/accounts/leeland/index.html* features current pro-

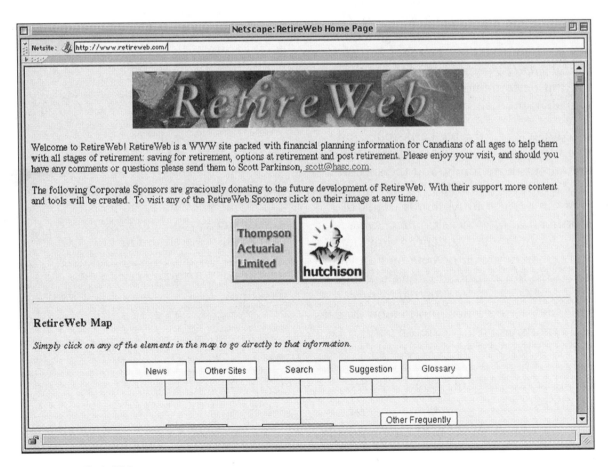

Figure 6.14 RetireWeb

jects, WWW resources and other information.

- Sagit Investment Management at *http://www.sagit.com/funds* provides aggressive and conservative fund information as well as additional information.

- Security APL at *http://www.secapl.com* provides a comprehensive Internet investment resource that features integrated portfolio accounting, securities and market research tools, real-time quotations, and online trading. There is also an extensive Website devoted to providing information to the investment advisory industry.

- Scudder Funds of Canada at *http://www.scudder.ca* discusses markets, seminars and fund profiles.

- The Mutual Group at *http://www.themutualgroup.com* has a Web site that summarizes a wide range of financial products and services.

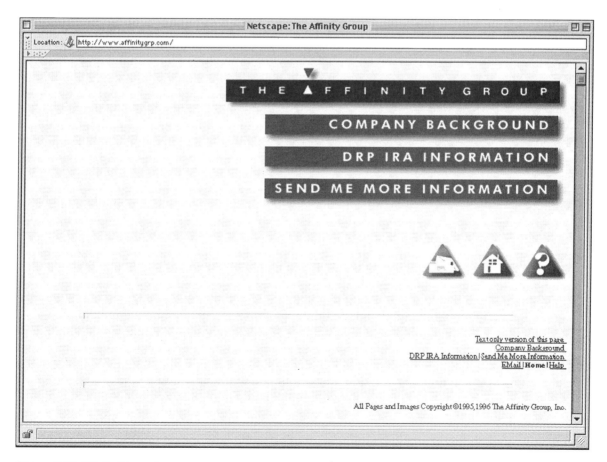

Figure 6.15 *Affinity Group Inc.*

FINANCIAL SOFTWARE AND UTILITIES

In addition to the number of sites we have addressed previously, there are also a number of independent sites that have developed software and other utilities that might be useful. Following is a synopsis of what is available at this time.

- BellCharts Inc at *http://www.bellcharts.com* allows you to study almost every fund sold in Canada on 30 columns of information, comparing, sorting, and ranking the funds by performance, size, manage-

ment expense ratios, volatility, and many more variables.

- ChartSmart at *http://www.chartsmart.com* covers virtually all stocks on the VSE, ASE, and TSE, providing over 3500 charts.

- Fimetrics Systems Ltd. at *http:// www.fimetrics.com* takes your estimates of future assets (salary, capital gain, CPP, etc.) and calculates an investment schedule which forces out a smooth net income. The result is a schedule of pay-

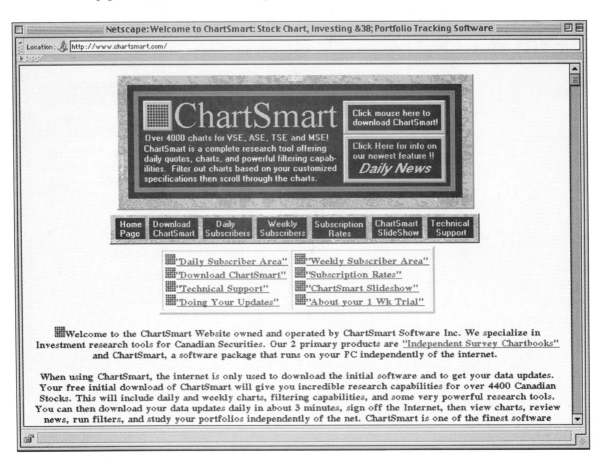

Figure 6.16 ChartSmart

ments, in, out, and between the two (registered and non-registered) capital pools.

- Primate Software at *http://primate.com* sells software to allow access to Primate's data base containing over 130,000 symbols on stocks (including bulletin board), bonds, mutual funds, indices, futures and options.

- RRIFmetic at *http://www.fimetrics.com* is a program that specializes in Canadian RRIF programs. It takes your estimates of future assets (salary, capital gain, CPP, etc.) and calculates an investment sched-

ule which forces out a smooth net income. The result is a schedule of payments, in, out, and between the two (registered and non-registered) capital pools. See Fimetrics Systems Ltd.

- Ten Star Term Quoter at *http://www.termquoter.com* contains the insurance rates of over 40 life insurance companies. This program is very user friendly. Enter your age, sex and smoking status plus the amount of life insurance you require; it will instantly calculate how much each life insurance company charges and automatically compare the cost for you!

SUMMARY OF WEB SITES MENTIONED IN CHAPTER 6

Name/Address

Canadian Financial Network Inc
http://www.CanadianFinance.COM/cfnbase/cdnbase.htm

Financial Information Link Library
http://www.mbnet.mb.ca/~russell

Finance Net
http://www.financenet.com

The Financial Post
http://www.canoe.com/FP/home.html

The Globe and Mail
http://www.globeandmail.ca

Infoglobe
http://qsilver.queensu.ca/law/infoglob.htm

Southam Newspapers
http://www.southam.com

Infomart
http://www.infomart.ca

Canada NewsWire Ltd
http://www.newswire.ca

Canadian Corporate News
http://www.cdn-news.com

Canadian Society of Technical Analysis
http://www.csta.org

StockHouse
http://www.stockhouse.com

Toronto Society of Financial Analysts
http://www.aimr.org/aimr/societies/local/toronto.html

Association for Investment Management and Research (AIMR)
http://www.aimr.org

Standard & Poor's Compustat
http://www.compustat.com

Canadian Industry Overviews
http://strategis.ic.gc.ca/sc_ecnmy/sio/homepage.html

Canadian Investor Relations and Corporate Communications
http://www.fin-info.com

Micromedia Ltd.
http://www.mmltd.com/files/homepage.html

Canadian Oil and Gas Financial Data Base
http://www.mopssr.com

Robertson Info-Data Inc.
http://www.info-mine.com

StockWatch.com
http://www.canada-stockwatch.com

Canadian Bankers Association
http://www.cba.ca/eng/index.htm

Bank of Montreal
http://www.bmo.com

Royal Bank of Canada
http://www.royalbank.com

Toronto Dominion Bank
http://www.tdbank.ca/tdbank

Scotiabank
http://www.scotiabank.ca

Canadian Imperial Bank of Commerce
http://www.cibc.com

Laurentian Bank of Canada
http://www.laurentianbank.com

Banca Commerciale Italiana of Canada
http://www.bcibank.ca

Business Development Bank of Canada
http://www.bdc.ca/bdc/home/index.html

Credit Union Central of Canada
http://www.cucentral.ca/home.html

Links to Canadian Credit Unions
http://www.cucentral.ca/provcuc/index.html

Credit Union Atlantic
http://www.cua.com

Credit Union Central Ontario
http://www.cuco.on.ca

Credit Unions of Saskatchewan
http://www.saskcu.com

Manitoba's Credit Unions
http://www.creditunion.mb.ca

Surrey Metro Savings Credit Union
http://www.metrosavings.com

Alberta Treasury Branches
http://www.atb.com

Latvian Credit Union Ltd.
http://www.lcu.homesite.ca

Mt. Lehman Credit Union
http://www.mtlehman.com

Toronto Electrical Utilities Credit Union
http://www.teucu.com

Assiniboia Credit Union
http://www.cypronet.com/~acu/info.html

Bergengren Credit Union
http://www.bergengrencu.com

Altamira
http://www.altamira.com

Fidelity Mutual Funds
http://www.fid-inv.com

Wood Gundy PCI
http://www.woodgundypci.com/home/index.html

Investment Brokerages Guide
http://www.cs.cmu.edu/~jdg/invest_brokers

MC&A Net Broker
http://www.netaxis.qc.ca.cma

Midland Walwyn
http://www.midwal.ca

Nesbitt Burns
http://www.bmo.com

RBC Dominion Securities Inc.
http://www.rbcds.com

Scotia Capital Markets
http://www.scotiacapital.com

The Canadian Institute of Financial Planning
http://www.mutfunds.com/cifp

Canadian Association of Financial Planners
http://www.cafp.org

Canadian Financial Advisory Service
http://cfas.com

Selecting a Financial Planner–Better Business Bureau
http://www.bbb.org

Canadian Mutual Fund Library
http://www.fundlib.com

Financial Service Network
http://www.fsn.ca/cgi-bin/DisplayPage?fsn@5.0

Fundata Canada Inc.
http://www.fundata.com

First Canadian Mutual Funds (Bank of Montreal
http://www.fcfunds.bomil.ca

Royal Mutual Funds
http://www.royalbank.com/english/rmf

TD Bank's Mutual Fund Centre
http://www.tdbank.ca/mutualfund

Investment Funds Institute of Canada
http://www.mutfunds.com/ific

Investment Challenge
http://inv-chal.yorku.ca

RetireWeb
http://www.retireweb.com

Affinity Group Inc.
http://www.affinitygrp.com

AGF Group of Funds
http://www.agf.com

Altamira Investment Services Inc.
http://www.altamira.com

Dynamic Mutual Funds
http://www.dynamic.ca

Fidelity Mutual Funds
http://www.fid-inv.com

Investors Group
http://www.investorsgroup.com

Leeland Financial Group
http://www.cadvision.com/Home_Pages/accounts/leeland/index.html

Sagit Investment Management
http://www.sagit.com/funds

Security APL
http://www.secapl.com

Scudder Funds of Canada
http://www.scudder.ca

The Mutual Group
http://www.themutualgroup.com

BellCharts Inc
http://www.bellcharts.com

ChartSmart
http://www.chartsmart.com

Fimetrics Systems Ltd.
http://www.fimetrics.com

Primate Software
http://primate.com

RRIFmetic
http://www.fimetrics.com

Ten Star Term Quoter
http://www.termquoter.com

7 GOVERNMENT AND TAXATION

INTRODUCTION

Accountants need information about many aspects of governments and their policies. First, of course, is taxation of all types—from income to commodity to the GST. But they also need information about government policies affecting business, the latest statistics and economic data, government grants, and other programs that might assist entrepreneurs.

In this chapter, we identify the most significant government sites likely to be of interest to accountants. We also document several non-governmental sites that provide useful information about government policies and programs.

THE CANADIAN GOVERNMENT

The Canadian government Web site at *http://canada.gc.ca/main_e.html* is an essential starting point for Canadian accountants who have a need for information about government departments, policies, and recent events. It contains reports from Statistics Canada, the Department of Finance, and exchange rates from the Bank of Canada. The information it makes available about individual departments and agencies and their programs and publications is truly comprehensive.

Take a look, for example, at the Web sites of Statistics Canada at *http://www.statcan.ca/start.html*, Revenue Canada at *http://www.rc.gc.ca/*, and the Department of Finance at *http://www.fin.gc.ca* to name just some of the sites most likely to be of greatest interest to accountants.

The Statistics Canada site contains sections on the daily news, financial indicators, latest census figures and access to Statcan publications and products. The daily news section has the latest information about the Consumer Price Index, labour force stats and economic indicators.

The Revenue Canada site offers information on a wide variety of matters dealing with taxes. Revenue Canada forms are available through this site and most Revenue Canada publications are available online.

The site of the Federal Department of Finance provides information about the initiatives of the department in guiding the broad economic affairs of the country. It has news releases, federal budgets, publications, and information about the Canada Pension Plan and the financial services sector of the economy. One of the strengths of this site is the many useful links to other Web sites pertinent to banks and financial institutions, corporate finance, economics, and international trade and finance.

Other departments and agencies of the Government of Canada can be found by consulting the menus on the main Government of Canada site.

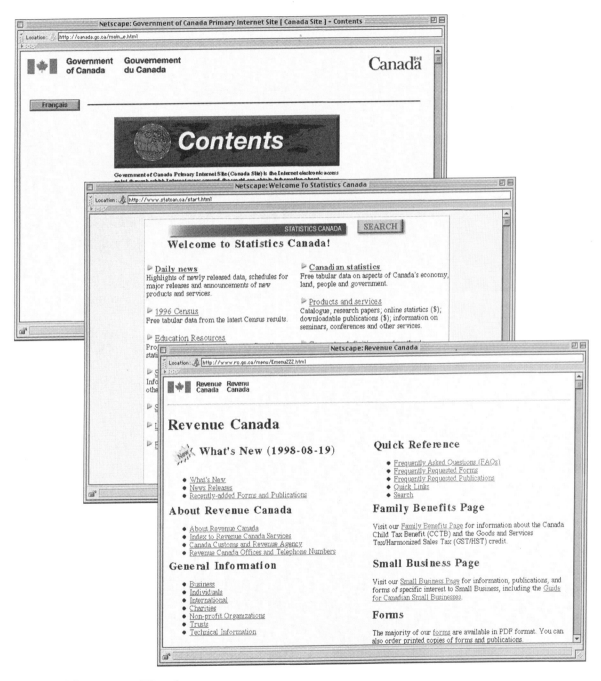

Figure 7.1 *Government of Canada*
Figure 7.2 *Statistics Canada*
Figure 7.3 *Revenue Canada*

Web sites of all provinces and territories can easily be found through the Canadian Government site from a link on the homepage to Provincial and Territorial Governments at *http://canada.gc.ca/othergov/prov_e.html*. The provincial Web sites generally provide a reasonable trail or indexing system to enable items of interest to be easily found.

MUNICIPAL GOVERNMENTS

Municipal governments, of course, come in all shapes and sizes. And there are too many to mention in a single publication. However, a few good lists are available on the Web that can be used to find them. Of course, a standard search engine can be used quite effectively in searching for a particular municipality. Entering "Municipality of Toronto", for example, will yield a result that will list the homepage of The New City of Toronto at *http://www.metrotor.on.ca*. A similar approach will often lead to satisfactory results. Montreal has a site called Communauté Urbaine de Montréal at *http://www.cum.qc.ca/index.html*.

Another way to find the Web pages of municipal governments is to use one of the lists of links available. There is one called Canada—Municipal Governments at *http://www.lib.uwaterloo.ca/discipline/*

Government/can_cities.html that provides good links. Many of the links are provided through the other major linklist at *http://www.intergov.gc.ca* that is quite comprehensive, although often busy.

INTERNATIONAL GOVERNMENTS

In a world of increasing global business, the Web sites of several foreign governments are likely to be of interest to Canadian accountants. It is impossible to list all of them, but certain countries stand out.

The United States, for example, has many obvious ties to Canadian business—so much so that the US is not treated as a foreign country in this book. However, this is a good place to mention the US government Web sites, that are numerous and can be difficult to sort through. In view of this difficulty, why not go right to the top to The White House at *http://www.whitehouse.gov*. On that site are many useful links of interest to accountants, including an excellent resource called the US Business Advisor at *http://www.business.gov*. Some of the other US sources have been mentioned in the chapters on accounting and auditing. Most of the important sites to accountants can be found through this service, such as the Web site of the Internal Revenue Service at *http://www.irs.ustreas.gov* and that of the

Federal Trade Commission at *http:// www.ftc.gov*. We have already mentioned the SEC site and others in preceding chapters.

Britain also has many ties to Canada and has Web sites at *http://www.open.gov.uk*. Other countries either have official Web sites or there are Web sites that contain much useful information about their government environments. For example, infor-

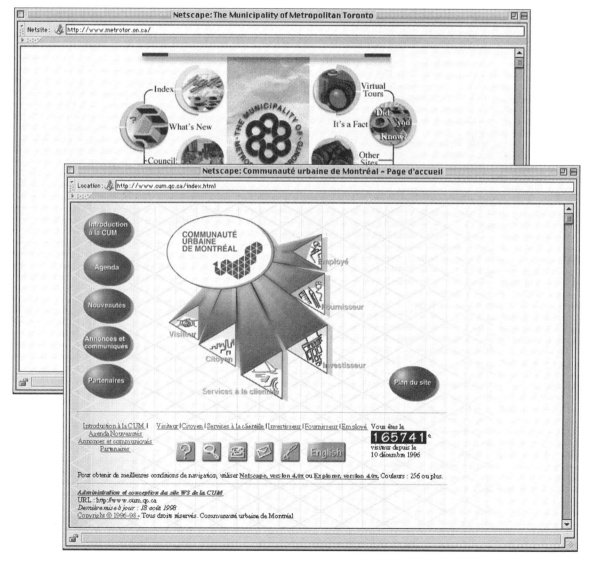

Figure 7.4 *The New City of Toronto*
Figure 7.5 *Communauté urbaine de Montréal*

mation on France can be found at *http://www.france.com*, Germany at *http://www.auswaertiges-amt.government.de*, the Netherlands at *http://www.minbiza.nl*, Japan at *http://www.mpt.go.jp*, Singapore at *http://www.ncb.gov.sg*, and Hong Kong at *http://www.info.gov.hk*.

Those with an interest in European policy can refer to the site of The Institute for

Figure 7.6 *The White House*
Figure 7.7 *US Business Advisor*

Fiscal Studies (IFS), which is one of Europe's pre-eminent centres of policy research. The site is at *http://www1.ifs.org.uk/index.htm*. The site provides information relating to policy development in Europe. Also contained within IFS is the ESRC Centre for Fiscal Policy.

A comprehensive site for finding national sites on the web is located at *http://champlain.gns.ca/opengov/world.html*.

TAX INFORMATION

Some accountants have more interest in taxes than others, but most pay taxes of some kind themselves, and therefore some interest at least cannot be totally avoided. Keeping up with taxes and other regulations can be a time consuming and difficult task.

There is a good deal of information on the Internet about taxes, some of it coming from authoritative government sources

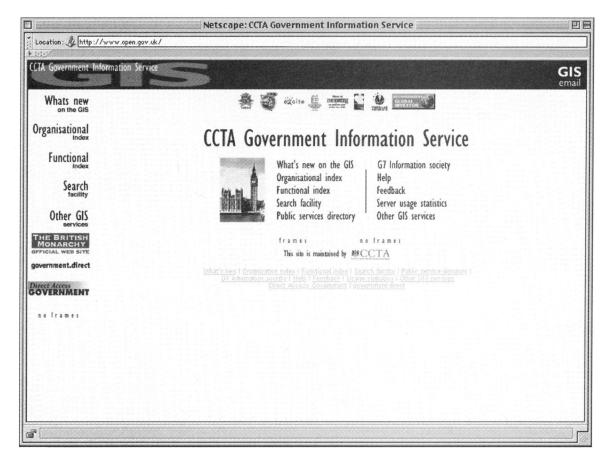

Figure 7.8 *Great Britian*

and some coming from private sources. Information is available about tax planning, policy, and information that can be useful in filing a tax return.

A prime source for authoritative and useful information is the Web site of Revenue Canada at *http://www.rc.gc.ca*. This important site has information dealing with "What's New" as well as a section on frequently asked questions (FAQs). Publications, guides and forms of the department are available through this page,

as are Revenue Canada Office addresses and telephone listings. Finally, the site includes a section on tax statistics.

Within the section on guides and forms can be found much of the most useful information for actually preparing tax returns or assisting others with that burdensome process. The General Income Tax Guides for various recent years are available at *http://www.rc.gc.ca/menu/ EmenuLZZ.html*.

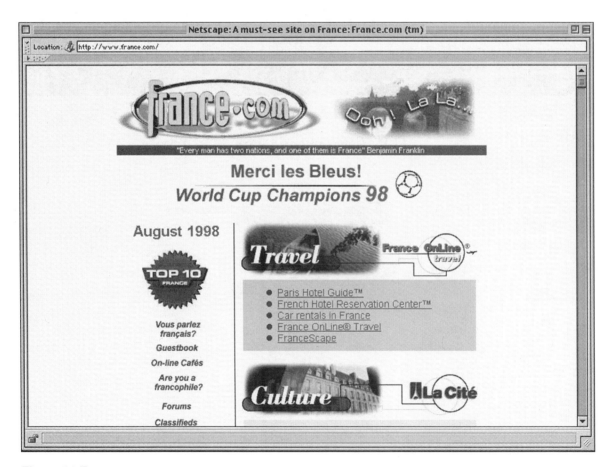

Figure 7.9 *France*

For US income tax forms, the IRS offers forms and publications at *http://www.irs.ustreas.gov*. Also, there is a site called Fedworld at *http://www.fedworld.gov* which provides access to several US forms.

Advance income tax rulings (ATRs) are also provided in the Revenue Canada site at *http://www.rc.gc.ca/menu/EmenuKZZ.html*, although it is just as easy to go to these items through the menu system on the main page of the Revenue Canada site.

Another good source of information about income taxes, including tax planning considerations, is in the Web sites of the major public accounting firms. For example, the site of KPMG at *http://www.kpmg.ca/tax* includes a "Tax Online" selection that provides a wealth of good information including various planning tips and the "Tip of the Day", as well as other features.

An excellent source of income tax information can also be found at Carswell–Thomson Professional Publishing at *http://www.carswell.com*. That site provides both a free and a commercial online service. As part of the free site, they provide a payroll community Web site, federal budget payroll news, a link to Revenue Canada's site for forms, and the TaxPartner newsletter called "Doublespeed".

Their commercial service, TAXNET, at *http://taxnet.carswell.com*, was voted "Best New Legal Online Product" by *Information Highways* magazine in 1997. This paid membership service provides a number of features including:

- a bulletin board service that provides full text of current press releases, information circulars, interpretation bulletins, tax decisions, and rulings;

- search/browse access to all Carswell tax databases including TaxPartner, GST Partner and Provincial Tax Partner;

- links to other professional sites;

- daily email delivery of tax news headlines of interest to practitioners with a direct link to the full text of the document on TAXNET.

For the payment of a membership fee, one can also make use of The Virtual Tax Resource Centre at *http://www.tax.ca* which is a joint venture of Ernst & Young and the CICA. It also contains a good deal of useful resource information, including a detailed newsletter, tax forms, rulings, etc. One of the services, TaxCast, provides the latest developments in Canadian tax (customs, excise/GST/HST, income, and provincial). Another service provides access to four tax and related information databases.

Of course, CCH has long been a standard reference for Canadian tax accountants. CCH Canadian has a Web site at *http://www.ca.cch.com* which provides information on what's new, industry tips and tidbits, and recent product announcements. It also has an online catalogue for ordering CCH publications. CCH's new Internet product, Protos on the Web, at *http://iworks.ca.cch.com/protos* provides the latest tax developments for paying subscribers.

TAX PREPARATION SOFTWARE

Taxprep Information Systems, provider of the popular tax preparation program, Taxprep, has a Web site at *http://www.taxprep.com*. The site offers extensive information about Taxprep, including a support facility. It also includes information about other products of the company.

Another popular tax preparation software product is CANTAX Income Tax Software, that has a Web site at *http://www.cantax.com*. This site contains infor-

mation about the product, as well as support and discussion forum capabilities.

For some other possibilities, take a look at Dr Tax at *http://www.drtax.ca*, GriffTax at *http://www.grifftax.com*. and Taxbyte at *http://www.taxbyte.com*. All provide a wide range of Canadian tax preparation software for Windows, some for tax professionals and others for just about any tax return preparer.

Freeware tax preparation software is available at *http://www.cooltax.com/*. Some peo-

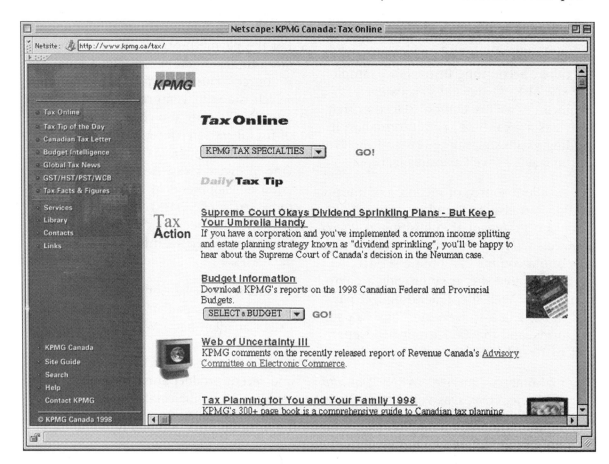

Figure 7.10 KPMG Canada

ple have used this product successfully and it is described as running on Windows 95 or NT. Windows 3.1 is no longer supported.

COMMODITY TAXES

Information on the dreaded Goods and Services Tax (GST) and Harmonized Sales Tax (HST) can be found in places similar to income taxes. Again the Revenue Can-

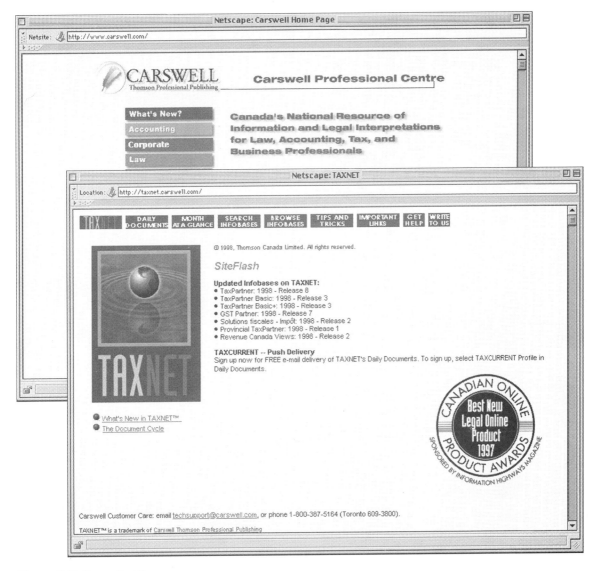

Figure 7.11 *Carswell—Thomson*
Figure 7.12 *TAXNET*

ada site has excellent useful and practical information at its Web site at *http://www.rc.gc.ca/menu/EmenuKZZ.html*. Information at the site includes GST/HST guides, pamphlets, forms, news, and changes in the GST.

Also, as with income taxes, valuable information is being provided by a number of Canadian firms of chartered accountants as well as the pay sites that were discussed earlier in this chapter, e.g., TAX-NET, Tax Cast, and Protos on the Web.

Figure 7.13 CCH Canadian Ltd.
Figure 7.14 Taxprep Information Systems

GOVERNMENT GRANTS

Considerable information about government grants is available on the Internet. There are several sites outlining federal grant programs, most notably, of course, the Government of Canada site at *http://canada.gc.ca*. That site contains a complete listing of all of the programs that are currently available for businesses. In addition, it includes a site for the Business Development Bank of Canada at *http://www.bdc.ca*.

Significant information is available about various Regional Economic Development Agencies, including the Atlantic Canada Opportunities Agency (ACOA) at *http://www.acoa.ca*, the Federal Economic Development Initiative for Northern Ontario (FedNor) at *http://strategis.ic.gc.ca/fednor/engdoc/homepage.html*, the Federal Office of Regional Development—Quebec (FORD-

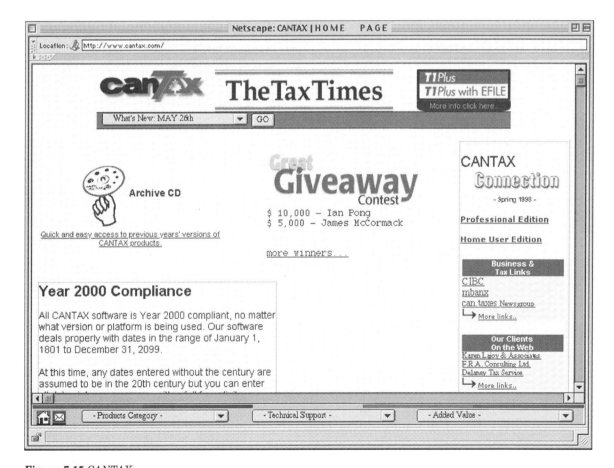

Figure 7.15 CANTAX

Q) at *http://www.cbsc.org/fedbis/bis/federal.html,* and the Western Economic Diversification Canada (WD) at *http://www.wd.gc.ca/eng/content/network/index.html.*

Industry Canada provides a good list of links to various programs at *http://strategis.ic.gc.ca/engdoc/main.html.* Other information about provincial aid programs can be found at the provincial Web sites mentioned above.

SUMMARY OF WEB SITES MENTIONED IN CHAPTER 7

Name/Address

Government of Canada
http://www.canada.gc.ca/main_e.html

Statistics Canada
http://www.statcan.ca/start.html

Revenue Canada
http://www.rc.gc.ca

Department of Finance
http://www.fin.gc.ca

Provincial and Territorial Governments
http://www.canada.gc.ca/othergov/prov_e.html

The New City of Toronto
http://www.metrotor.on.ca

Communauté Urbaine de Montréal
http://www.cum.qc.ca/index.html

Canada—Municipal Governments
http://www.lib.uwaterloo.ca/discipline/Government/can_cities.html

Link list of government sites
http://www.intergov.gc.ca

The White House
http://www.whitehouse.gov

US Business Advisor
http://www.business.gov

US Internal Revenue Service
http://www.irs.ustreas.gov

US Federal Trade Commission
http://www.ftc.gov

Britain
http://www.open.gov.uk

France
http://www.france.com

Germany
http://www.auswaertiges-amt.government.de

Netherlands
http://www.minbiza.nl

Japan
http://www.mpt.go.jp

Singapore
http://www.ncb.gov.sg

Hong Kong
http://www.info.gov.hk

Institute for Fiscal Studies (UK)
http://www1.ifs.org.uk/index.htm

National governments on the Web
http://champlain.gns.ca/opengov/world.html

Revenue Canada Guides and Forms
http://www.rc.gc.ca/menu/EmenuKZZ.html

US income tax forms—IRS
http://www.irs.ustreas.gov

Fedworld
http://www.fedworld.gov

KPMG
http://www.kpmg.ca/tax

Carswell Publications
http://www.carswell.com

TAXNET
http://taxnet.carswell.com

The Virtual Tax Resource Centre
http://www.tax.ca

CCH Canadian
http://www.ca.cch.com

Protos on the Web
http://iworks.ca.cch.com/protos

Taxprep Information Systems
http://www.taxprep.com

CANTAX Tax Software
http://www.cantax.com

Dr Tax
http://www.drtax.ca

GriffTax
http://www.grifftax.com

Taxbyte
http://www.taxbyte.com

Cooltax
http://www.cooltax.com

GST and HST information
http://www.rc.gc.ca/menu/EmenuKZZ.html

Business Development Bank of Canada
http://www.bdc.ca

Atlantic Canada Opportunities Agency (ACOA)
http://www.acoa.ca

Federal Economic Development Initiative for Northern Ontario (FedNor)
http://strategis.ic.gc.ca/fednor/engdoc/homepage.html

Federal Office of Regional Development—Quebec (FORD-Q)
http://www.cbsc.org/fedbis/bis/federal.html

Western Economic Diversification Canada (WD)
http://www.wd.gc.ca/eng/content/network/index.html

Industry Canada
http://strategis.ic.gc.ca/engdoc/main.html

8 INFORMATION TECHNOLOGY

INTRODUCTION

GETTING ASSISTANCE AT THE START

HARDWARE SALES AND SUPPORT
NEW COMPUTER SALES AND SUPPORT
USED COMPUTER STORES
CATALOGUE SALES

APPLICATION SOFTWARE

AUDITING SOFTWARE

SPECIAL PROBLEMS
VIRUSES
YEAR 2000

COMPUTER SECURITY
ADDITIONAL SECURITY INFORMATION

COMPUTER LITERATURE
SPECIFIC INFORMATION FOR THE ACCOUNTANT
OTHER
SOME COLLECTION SITES

SOME BIG LINK SITES

SUMMARY OF WEB SITES MENTIONED IN CHAPTER 8

INTRODUCTION

Because it relies on technology and is quickly becoming a favoured site to sell software and hardware, the Internet has become an important vehicle for obtaining computer-related information.

The purpose of this chapter is to discuss how accountants can use the Internet to find technological information in a number of areas including, but not limited to, online technological assistance, be it for Year 2000 information, software upgrades (or patches), finding out what hardware is setting, or anticipated to set, performance standards, or to answer questions that one might have about Internet risks. It will also set out a number of site links that are all-encompassing.

the potential use of this resource. You should refer to "overview to the Web" site, maintained by Webmaster at *http://www.cio.com/WebMaster/sem2_home.html*. It has detailed information as well as references and links to other sites that have important resources and plug-ins that might be needed to effectively use some of the files that can be downloaded. InfoRamp, Inc. has an excellent general help site at *http://kato.theramp.net/inforamp/new_user.html*. This site has links to shareware and information to help a new user as much as possible.

Your Internet service provider should also provide some valuable assistance. For example, Istar provides some excellent assistance at their "super help" site at *http://www.istar.ca/html/supportframset.html*. Most Internet service providers should offer some basic help to get you started.

GETTING ASSISTANCE AT THE START

To make sure you have all of the programs you need, look under "help" in Netscape for software and plug-ins for assistance at *http://www.netscape.com/computing/index.html?cp=hom07ccom*. You will then see, on the left hand menu, a section for downloading software, plug-ins, browsers, etc. to your computer.

There is excellent help for the novice user that has signed on and is not quite sure of

HARDWARE SALES AND SUPPORT

Many of the significant hardware manufacturers now have sites where they provide product information and, in some cases, even sell on line. Most of the significant vendors can be reached through Internet sites, using their corporate name as the search string in one of the more powerful search engines (Lycos or AltaVista) to get their URL reference.

Following is an analysis of some of the sites that might be of interest.

NEW COMPUTER SALES AND SUPPORT

IBM Canada has sites worldwide, but it has a principal Canadian site at *http://www.can.ibm.com/*. It is an extensive site covering hardware, applications, software, support, Year 2000 solutions and other resources. There is also a French site that is available for many of the internal links (for example, the French version of PC hardware) at *http://www.can.ibm.com/pcco/francais/*.

Compaq Corporation, the world's largest seller of personal computers, has a bilingual Canadian site at *http://www.compaq.ca/*. It provides news, hardware information, repair assistance and other resources.

Apple Canada at *http://www.apple.ca/* provides news and event information, hardware and software information as well as

Figure 8.1 IBM Canada

user group information. It also has a French site at *http://www.apple.ca/fr/*.

The Canadian operations of Dell Corporation at *http://www.dell.com/intl/ca/index.htm* provides product and sales and service information as well as Dell Canada corporate information.

The Canadian operations of Toshiba, Toshiba of Canada Limited at *http:www.toshiba.ca* has a site that provides product and sales and service information as well as corporate information.

Packard Bell NEC Canada at *http://www.pbnec.ca/* provides product and sales and service information as well as corporate information.

Just Imagine at *http://www.justimagine.com/* sells PC clones out of its New Brunswick head office. They provide full product and pricing information and you have the option of ordering online or can leave a message for a representative to call you.

Gateway 2000 at *http://www.gateway2000.com/* is another mail or-

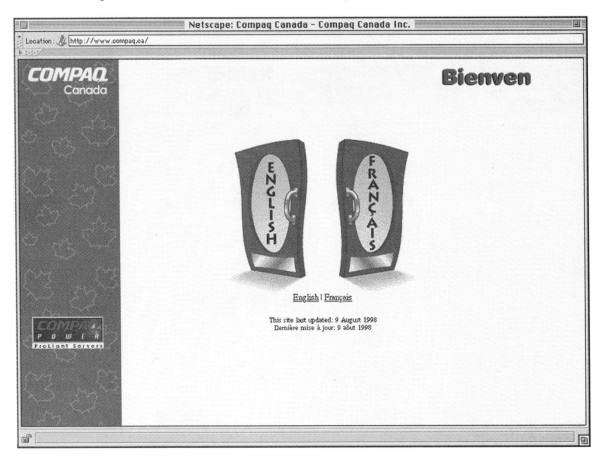

Figure 8.2 Compaq Canada

der computer company. The enterprise does not have a separate Canadian centre, but sells into Canada through its international sales division (US).

USED COMPUTER STORES

Although they are available at a number of sites, one of the more popular sites can be found at CPUsed in Toronto at *http://www.cpused.com/*. They have an online cat-

Figure 8.3 *Apple Canada*
Figure 8.4 *Just Imagine*

alogue for both Apple and Windows/DOS products.

CATALOGUE SALES

To get a current list, the significant search engines should be used. The more prominent ones for computer peripherals is MicroWarehouse at *http://www.warehouse.com/*. They sell all major types of hardware and software in a number of countries around the world. Another significant vendor is ISTAR Internet Catalogue at *http://www.comspec.com/webcat/index.html*.

Figure 8.5 *MicroWarehouse*

APPLICATION SOFTWARE

The significant computer applications are in word processing, spreadsheet, database, Internet, graphics and presentation software. Most of the major players in this market have software sales and support sites that can be accessed through the Internet.

Corel's purchase of WordPerfect from Novell and Corel's suite of products including WordPerfect for Windows and Quattro Pro has made it a major player in the application suite market in competition with Microsoft. It provides product and support information at *http:// www.corel.com or http:// www.wordperfect.com/*.

Lotus, now part of IBM, provides product support and information at *http:// www3.lotus.com/home.nsf*.

Microsoft Corporation, of course, needs no introduction due to its significance in the PC world. You are able to obtain product, support, and other information as well as free Internet software at their site at *http://www.microsoft.com/*.

Product and support of Novell, Inc.'s Netware and other products is located at *http://www.novell.com/*.

Adobe Systems Incorporated produces popular products, such as Pagemaker, Framemaker, Persuasion and Photoshop, among others. Its product, sales, support and other information can be found at *http://www.adobe.com/homepage.shtml*.

Netscape Communications Corporation, best known for its Internet navigator has its product and other information at *http://home.netscape.com/*.

AUDITING SOFTWARE

Two products dominate the auditing software market.

The Canadian Institute of Chartered Accountants sells Interactive Data Extraction and Analysis (IDEA), advertised as "the world's leading audit automation package" at *http://www.cica.ca/idea/index.htm*.

ACL sells a competing product. Its product, sales, and support information is available at *http://www.acl.com/*.

SPECIAL PROBLEMS

VIRUSES

One of the most significant problems with transferring files from computer to computer is the possibility of transferring a virus that permeates a corporate network. To prevent this from occurring, it is important to have virus protection. Two of the significant suppliers in this industry

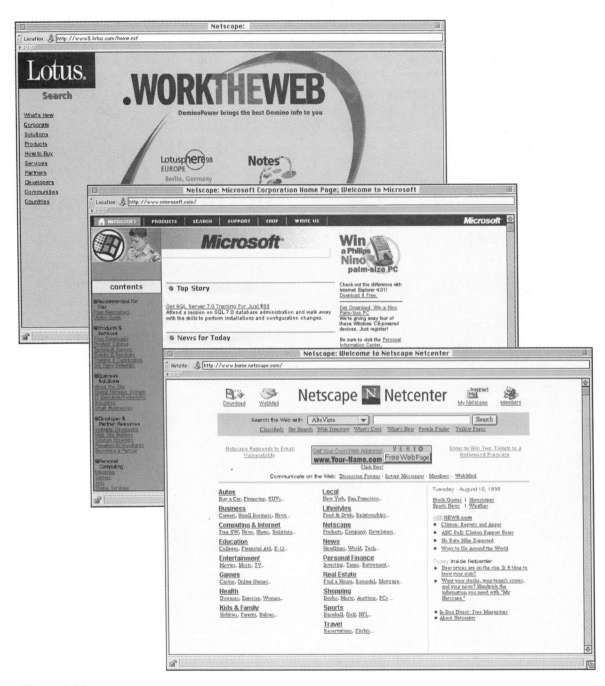

Figure 8.6 *Lotus*
Figure 8.7 *Microsoft*
Figure 8.8 *Netscape Communications*

are MacAfee at *http://www.mcafee.com* and Norton Utilities at *http://www.symantec.ca/*. Both offer sales through the Internet as well as the potential to update virus definitions at no cost from their Internet sites. This will allow the user to make sure that there is protection against all of the most current viruses.

There are a number of other virus software packages that are available. You can do a search on AltaVista or any of the other engines using the string (vi-

rus+detection+software) and get approximately 300 hits which can be investigated for other packages. The search string can be increased to include the platform that you are using to get more specific applications.

YEAR 2000

One of the most significant problems facing clients in the next few years is the Year 2000 problem, the potential for a number of computers and operation sys-

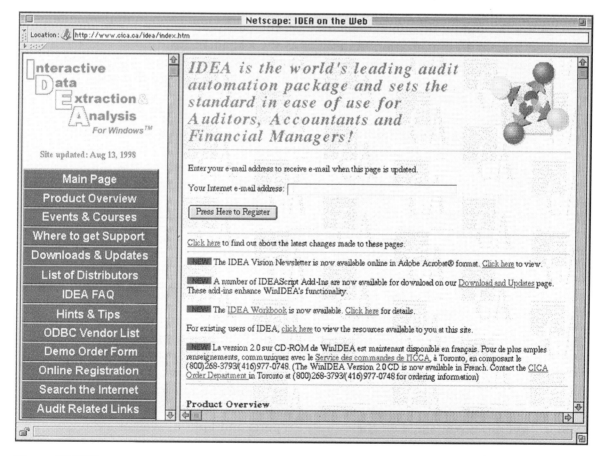

Figure 8.9 CICA

tems ceasing to work when the date January 1, 2000 is reached. When January 1, 2000 is received as data input to a computer program, many of the world's computers will assume that the year 1900, not 2000, has been reached. This issue is largely due to the computer misinterpreting a two-digit year date and problems in hardware that cannot accept a four-digit year date.

The costs to fix this problem have been estimated at up to $600 billion by the Gartner Group. There are a number of sources on the Internet that provide assistance, in the form of information supplier references, to help an organization understand the problem and how to fix it. To surf the WWW in respect of this issue, one should use the search string "year+2000+computer" or "y2k+computer" to get a large number of sites.

Year 2000 Information Network at *http://www.mbs-program.com* has a bulletin board for discussion and provides articles, news and other Year 2000 site links.

The National Bulletin Board for the Year 2000 at *http://www.it2000.com/* also provides a bulletin board and extensive news, articles and forums on this issue.

Larry Towner's Year 2000 Bibliography at *http://www.ttuhsc.edu/pages/year2000/y2k_bib.htm* provides an extensive database of articles on Year 2000. They are indexed by author and title. Hot links are provided to articles contained on the Internet.

The Year 2000 Information Centre maintained by Peter de Jager is viewed by many as a pre-eminent site. This site at *http://www.year2000.com* provides a bulletin board and extensive news, articles, and links to other sites that deal with this issue.

Department of Information Services' (DIS) Year 2000 Project Information Resource Center at *http://www.wa.gov/dis/2000/y2000.htm* provides articles, hardware and software compliance surveys, links, acquisition information and other information.

In the past year, accounting bodies such as the Canadian Institute of Chartered Accountants have established Year 2000 sites for providing guidance to members on Year 2000 issues and for providing links to other notable sources. The site at *http://www.cica.ca* should be referred to by accountants for understanding their responsibilities with respect to this important issue. In the United States, the American Institute of Certified Public Accountants has provided information to their members at *http://www.aicpa.org*.

In addition, in the latter part of 1997, Industry Canada began a significant initiative to educate the Canadian public and business community about the seriousness of the Year 2000 issue in Canada. They have an excellent Web site at *http://strategis.ic.gc.ca/sc_mangb/y2k/burst.html* that should be referred to. It has copies of their task force reports, strategic partner reports and links as well as a directory for Year 2000 service providers.

Microsoft TechNet IT at *http://www.microsoft.com/ithome/default.htm* provides significant information about Year 2000. Also see *http://www.microsoft.com*.

Both IBM and Apple provide Year 2000 information in respect to their products. IBM's is at *http://www.ibm.com/IBM/year2000/* while Apple's information is at *http://www.apple.com/macos/info/2000.html*.

These are just a sample. Many developers deal with this issue as part of their WWW

site. The de Jager site should be a starting point for Year 2000.

COMPUTER SECURITY

There are a number of organizations that provide information on how to protect

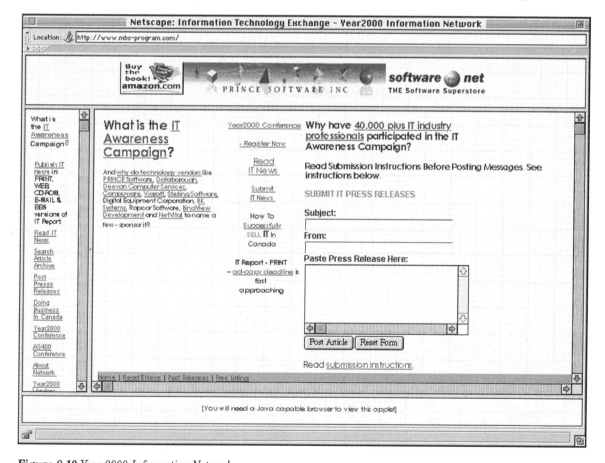

Figure 8.10 *Year 2000 Information Network*

computers and electronic transmission of information. One of the best places to start is at *http://www.yahoo.com/ Computers//*. It provides various categories from which one could choose. Some of the specific sites that should be referred to are listed below.

ADDITIONAL SECURITY INFORMATION

Internet Security Systems provides an excellent Unix and NT security library at *http://www.iss.net/vd/library.html*.

The CERT* Coordination Centre was formed in 1988 to serve as a focal point for the computer security concerns of Internet users. It studies Internet security vulnerabilities, provides incident response services to sites that have been the victims of attack, publishes a variety of security alerts, researches security and survivability in wide-area-networked computing, and develops information to help users improve security at their site The site is at *http://www.cert.org/*.

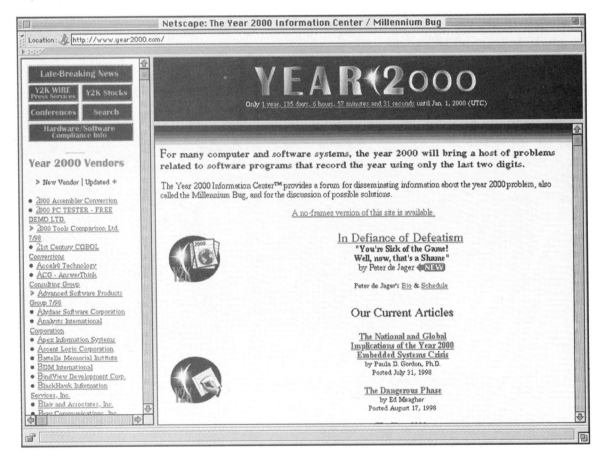

Figure 8.11 Year 2000 Information Centre

The National Security Institute's Security Resource Net provides a robust collection of information about security, Internet and otherwise at *http://www.nsi.org*. This site is an online information service from the National Security Institute. It's designed to provide a diverse range of security information consolidated under an umbrella Internet site. It is advertised as the premier Internet resource for the security industry. The site features industry and product news, computer alerts, travel advisories, a calendar of events, a directory of products and services, and access to an extensive virtual security library.

RSA's Data Security Homepage encryption is included in many commercial security standards. The RSA site at *http://www.rsa.com/* is a good source of security, privacy, and encryption information.

The International Computer Security Association, formerly the National Computer Security Association is an independent or-

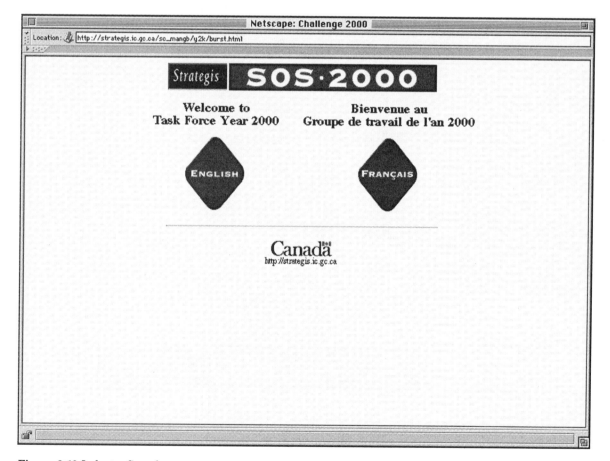

Figure 8.12 Industry Canada

ganization that promotes continuous improvement of commercial digital security through the application of their CSA Risk Framework and Continuous Certification Model to certification, research, and related activities. The organization is dedicated to continually improving global security, trust, and confidence in computing through the certification of products, systems, and people. Its site is at *http://www.ncsa.com/*.

The mission of TRUSTe is to establish trust and confidence in electronic transactions.

TRUSTe seeks to promote the mass adoption of electronic commerce by providing users with a trusted brand for privacy. The principles behind TRUSTe are disclosure and informed consent: when users visit a Web site, they will be informed of what information the site is gathering about them, what the site is doing with that information, and with whom that information is being shared. Their site is at *http://www.etrust.org/*.

VeriSign, Inc. is the leading provider of digital authentication services and prod-

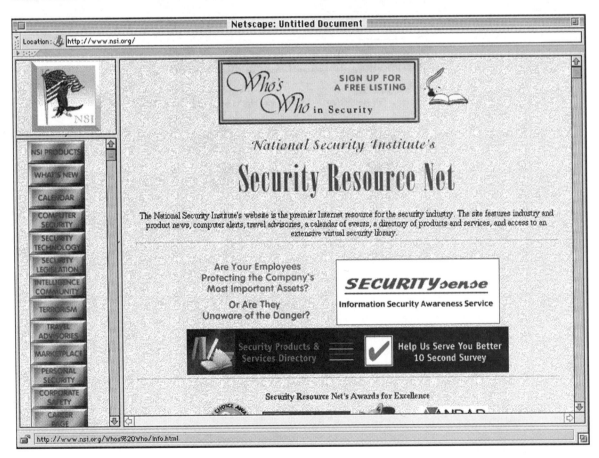

Figure 8.13. *National Security Institute's Security Resource Net*

ucts for electronic commerce and other forms of secure communications. Their site is at *http://www.verisign.com/*.

There are, of course, many organizations that deal with these issues that are located in Canada and the US. These are just a sample of the types of organizations that exist.

COMPUTER LITERATURE

The accountant will likely be interested in up-to-date literature that is provided in respect of hardware and software currently in use and in future technology directions. In this regard, there are a number of computer magazines that have online versions. Although there are hundreds of publications that could be accessed, it is important to just focus on the

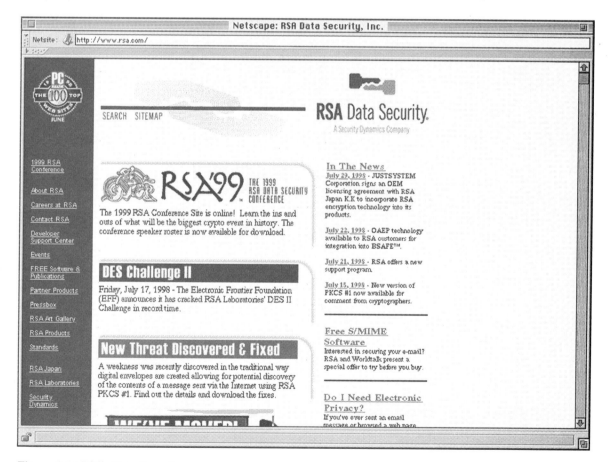

Figure 8.14 RSA's Data Security

most relevant ones. Some of the ones that should be reviewed are listed below.

SPECIFIC INFORMATION FOR THE ACCOUNTANT

The Electronic Accountant is one of the best in this area, providing a daily news-wire, discussions, feature articles, and links for accountants. It is maintained by Faulkner and Gray at *http://www.electronicaccountant.com/*. Much of it is

oriented towards the US CPA, but much of the information could be relevant to Canadian practitioners.

OTHER

AnchorDesk at *http://www4.zdnet.com/anchordesk/index.html* is an insider analysis of important computer news from Ziff-Davis.

Computer Currents Magazine at *http://www.currents.net/magazine/national/na-*

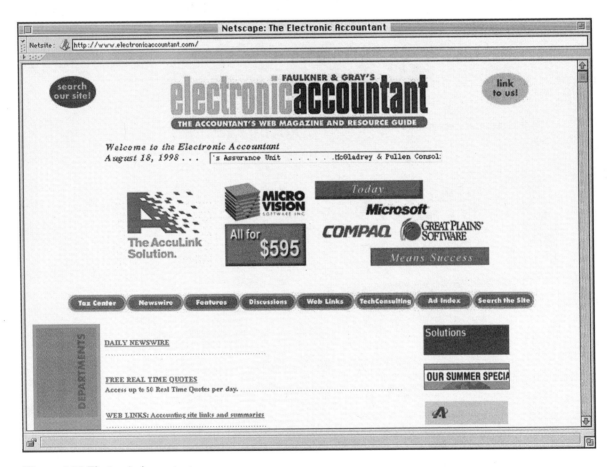

Figure 8.15 Electronic Accountant

tional.html provides some business information as well as other technology information.

Inter@ctive Week produced by Ziff-Davis, is located at *http://www.zdnet.com/intweek/*. It provides a synopsis of current Internet related business news.

Internet User, produced by Ziff-Davis, provides an excellent discussion of Internet technologies. It is at *http://www.netguide.com/home*.

NetGuide Magazine Online, produced by CMP Media, advertises itself as "The #1 source to everything on the Internet". It is at *http://techweb.cmp.com/ng/home/*.

NewsLinx at *http://newslinx.com/* provides a daily news feed on WWW events. It has a number of email topic groups available, including accounting, business, government, legal, etc. You can also subscribe to a software newsletter.

PC Magazine Online, produced by Ziff-Davis, provides excellent technology discussions and covers significant business events impacting technology. It is at *http://www8.zdnet.com/pcmag/*.

Windows Internet Magazine, produced by CMP Media, contains a number of news and technology articles, as well as a list of good download and other sites, referenced by subject (including business). The magazine site is at *http://www.winmag.com/* while downloads are available at *http://www.winmag.com/library/1997/0901/cover117.htm*.

SOME COLLECTION SITES

The Top 100 Computer Hardware and Software Magazines and Journals contains links to the top 100, organized alphabetically. It is an interesting site at *http://www.internetvalley.com/top100mag.html*.

WebCrawler Computer and Internet Channel at *http://my.excite.com/computers_webcrawler/computers_and_internet/?cobrand=webcrawler* is referenced to a number of channels as well as providing a news feature.

Yahoo! has an indexed list, by subject area at *http://www.yahoo.com/Computers_and_Internet/News_and_Media/Magazines//*. You can choose computer magazines, business, or other to take you to additional linked pages.

SOME BIG LINK SITES

In this chapter we have avoided relying on "mega-link" sites, concentrating on providing specific URLs instead. This avoids the problems of placing undue reliance on one site to provide all of the links that you might ever need in case that site is discontinued.

In the development of this chapter there were some notable sites that we encountered. First of all, there is the Computer Information Centre at *http://www.compinfo.co.uk/index.htm* that has been regarded as "The definitive directory of the Business side of Computing...It's among the top ten computing-specific sites we've ever seen"—Yahoo! Computing. It is an extensive resource for all facets of technology and is well worth bookmarking.

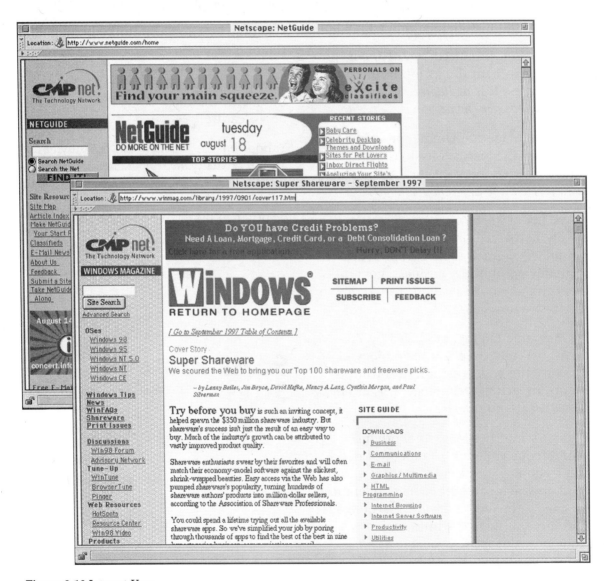

Figure 8.16 *Internet User*
Figure 8.17 *Windows Internet Magazine*

For magazines, one of the most extensive sites is located on the Three Rivers FREE-NET entitled Internet and Computer Magazines/News at *http://trfn.clpgh.org/Internet/magazines.html*. This site contains links to most of the magazines discussed in this chapter, as well as many others. Overall it is another site that is worth bookmarking for ongoing reference.

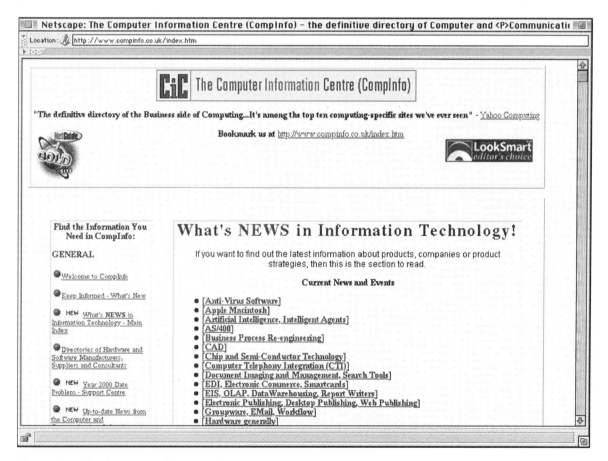

Figure 8.18 The Computer Information Centre

SUMMARY OF WEB SITES MENTIONED IN THIS CHAPTER

Name/Address

Netscape Communications Inc
http://www.netscape.com/

Webmaster
http://www.cio.com/WebMaster/sem2_home.html

InfoRamp, Inc.
http://kato.theramp.net/inforamp/new_user.html

Istar
http://www.istar.ca/html/supportframset.html

IBM Canada
http://www.can.ibm.com/

IBM Canada (French)
http://www.can.ibm.com/pcco/francais/

Compaq Corporation
http://www.compaq.ca/

Apple Canada
http://www.apple.ca/

Apple Canada (French)
http://www.apple.ca/fr/

Toshiba of Canada
http:www.toshiba.ca

Packard Bell NEC Canada
http://www.pbnec.ca

Dell Corporation
http://www.dell.com/intl/ca/index.htm

Just Imagine
http://www.justimagine.com

Gateway 2000
http://www.gateway2000.com/

CPUsed
http://www.cpused.com/

Microwarehouse
http://www.warehouse.com/

ISTAR Internet Catalogue
http://www.comspec.com/webcat/index.html

Corel
http://www.corel.com

Lotus
http://www3.lotus.com/home.nsf

Microsoft Corporation
http://www.microsoft.com/

Novell, Inc.
http://www.novell.com/

Adobe Systems Incorporated
http://www.adobe.com/homepage.html

The Canadian Institute of Chartered Accountants
http://www.cica.ca/idea/index.htm

ACL
http://www.acl.com

Year 2000 Information Network
http://www.mbs-program.com

The National Bulletin Board for the Year 2000
http://www.it2000.com/

Larry Towner's Year 2000 Bibliography
http://www.ttuhsc.edu/pages/year2000/y2k_bib.htm

The Year 2000 Information Centre™
http://www.year2000.com

Industry Canada
http://strategis.ic.gc.ca/sc_mangb/y2k/burst.html

Internet Security Systems
http://www.iss.net/vd/library.html

The CERT* Coordination Centre
http://www.cert.org/

National Security Institute
http://www.nsi.org

RSA's Data Security Homepage
http://www.rsa.com/

International Computer Security Association
http://www.ncsa.com/

TRUSTe
http://www.etrust.org/

VeriSign, Inc.
http://www.verisign.com/

The Electronic Accountant
http://www.electronicaccountant.com/

AnchorDesk
http://www4.zdnet.com/anchordesk/index.html

Computer Currents Magazine
http://www.currents.net/magazine/national/national.html

Inter@ctive Week
http://www.zdnet.com/intweek/

Internet User
http://www.netguide.com/home

NetGuide Magazine Online
http://techweb.cmp.com/ng/home/

NewsLinx
http://newslinx.com/

PC Magazine Online
http://www8.zdnet.com/pcmag/

Windows Internet Magazine
http://www.winmag.com/

The Top 100 Computer Hardware and Software Magazines and Journals
http://www.internetvalley.com/top100mag.html

WebCrawler Computer and Internet Channel
http://my.excite.com/computers_webcrawler/computers_and_internet/?cobrand=webcrawler

Yahoo! (business magazines)
http://www.yahoo.com/Computers_and_Internet/News_and_Media/Magazines/

Computer Information Centre
http://www.compinfo.co.uk/index.htm

Internet and Computer Magazines/News
http://trfn.clpgh.org/Internet/magazines.html

9 BUSINESS MANAGEMENT

BUSINESS MANAGEMENT SITES

In the field of management, there is no better place to start—some of the world's best managers did—than at the Harvard Business School. The HBS Web site at *http://www.hbs.edu* naturally outlines their educational programs, like the MBA and doctoral programs, but also provides extensive information about recent research and publications, including the *Harvard Business Review*.

And who could discuss management without mentioning Peter Drucker? Check out the Web site of the Peter F. Drucker Canadian Foundation at *http://www.drucker.com*. This foundation was established "to find the innovators, whether small or large; to recognize and celebrate their example; and to inspire others".

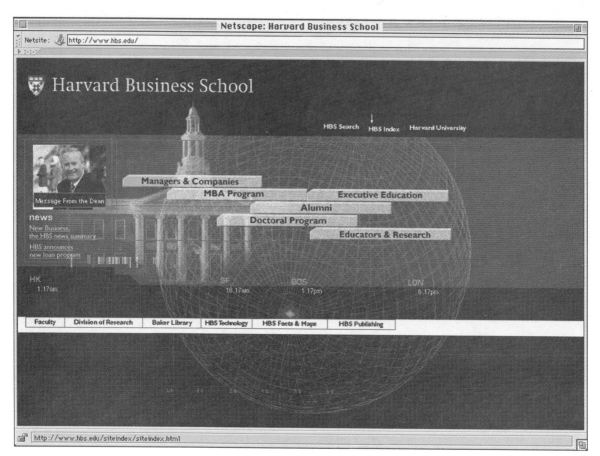

Figure 9.1 *Harvard Business School*

The purpose of the Peter F. Drucker Canadian Foundation is to call attention to the innovative and essential contributions to society by nonprofit organizations. The site provides a good deal of information about innovative thinking in management of non-profit organizations, and also links to Mr Drucker's books. The US site is found at *http://www.pfdf.org*.

The Peter F. Drucker Graduate Management Center of Claremont, California, has a Web site at *cgsweb.cgs.edu/drucker/page_*

one.html. The Center offers two degree-granting programs, primarily for practicing managers, the MBA Program, and the Executive Management Program. The site includes details about these programs.

Many associations of management exist, too many to mention here. However, we will attempt to identify some of the more useful association Web sites.

The American Management Association (AMA) International has a Web site at

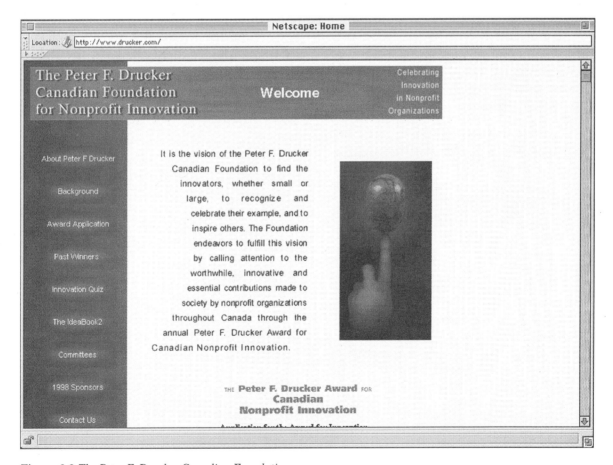

Figure 9.2 *The Peter F. Drucker Canadian Foundation*

http://www.amanet.org. The site contains references to "more than 200 seminars and video/interactive courses covering all areas of management and organizational development". These can be accessed through the Information Resource Center or the Books and Self-Study Resources icons.

The Canadian affiliate of the American Management Association International network, the Canadian Management Centre (CMC), has its site at *http://www.cmcamai.org*. This Centre is a leading training and development organization in the management area. Working in both the private and not-for-profit sectors, CMC draws upon the resources and expertise of AMA for its training and development activities.

It has a Presidents Association of Canada, which serves top executives through networking and management training programs. The CMC also offers customized on-site training, and through the government services division, offers management development solutions for the public sector.

The site also offers a wealth of resource material on topics of current interest. This includes the library from AMACOM Books, AMA's book publishing division. It also includes Trend Watch, the electronic newsletter of the AMA. It covers a wide range of business-related topics, is updated monthly, and has links to AMA publications and research reports.

One of the most prominent associations involved with management in Canada is the Certified Management Consultants Association. Their Web site at *http://www.cmc-consult.org* includes information about the role of certified management consultants as well as some technical information, such as information on ISO9000 requirements.

There are a variety of organizations that are essentially focused on a particular area. These sites would generally be of greatest interest to those directly involved in the speciality. Such sites include the Association for Systems Management (ASM), the International Facility Management Association, the National Association of Purchasing Management (NAPM), the Data Administration Management Association, the National Association of Credit Management (NACM), the Association of Information Systems Professionals (DPMA), the Purchasing Management Association of Canada (PMAC), the Canadian Credit Risk Management Association, the Management Software Association, the Business Forms Management Association, and the Chemical Resources & Management Association. All of these can be accessed easily by entering their names in a search engine such as Altavista at *http://www.altavista.digital.com* or Metacrawler at *http://metacrawler.com*.

PROJECT MANAGEMENT

As organizations make greater use of outsourcing particular projects, the area of project management has assumed tremendous importance in recent years. And, as they use project management techniques to optimize the use of scarce resouces for more efficient operations, project management has assumed the role of a mainstream management technique.

There are several organizations that have been formed to support project managers and that have Web sites. One of the most important is the Project Management Institute at *http://www.pmi.org*. This exceptional site provides discussion forums, information on careers, and numerous project management related links.

The Project Management Institute was founded in 1969, and since then has grown to over 28,500 members worldwide. It is widely considered the leading

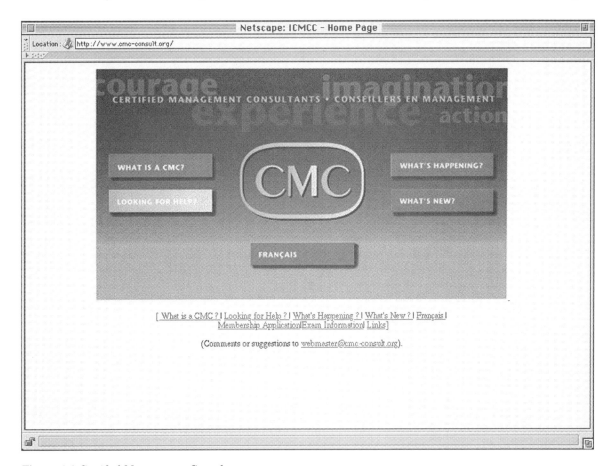

Figure 9.3 *Certified Management Consultants*

professional association in the field of project management. The Institute establishes project management standards, and provides seminars and other educational programs leading to certification as a Project Management Professional (PMP). In a world of growing use of project management, it fills a need for professionalism.

The site provides extensive material on issues of current interest, as well as PMI's mission statement, information on its standards, code of ethics, and other products and services.

Access to PMI publications through the PMI Bookstore is also provided through the site. In addition, there is a Project Management Network Online (PM Network) and information about the PM Journal. Finally, the site includes the complete Guide to the Project Management Body of Knowledge. (PMBOK Guide Online). For those interested or involved in

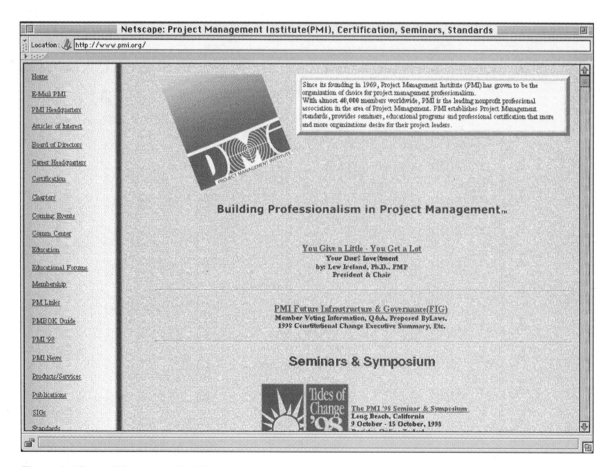

Figure 9.4 *Project Management Institute*

project management, the PMI site is a must.

Another professional organization, the Center for International Project and Program Management (CIPPM), is described in its Web site at *http://ireland.iol.ie/ ~mattewar/CIPPM* as "an international association and center of advanced communication, research, and learning for professional project managers and those interested in project management". The purpose of CIPPM is "to serve, support, and advance project and quality management which serves society, including public and private business, politics, and social".

CIPPM was founded in 1987 and is a non-profit organization based in Ann Arbor, Michigan at the University of Michigan. It has 6900 members, affiliates, and sponsors internationally. The organization supports the ethical guidelines as published by the Project Management Institute.

The CIPPM site provides information on ethics, membership, affliliation, sponsorship, and a variety of links to PM related sites. It is a good resource for project management information.

Another good project management resource is ProjectNet at *http:// www.projectnet.co.uk*. This UK site has some excellent detailed information on many aspects of project management, including case studies, products and demo software, and other timely information.

The tasks of project management are usually assisted with the use of project man-

agement software. Several products are on the market and an extremely comprehensive analysis of them is found on the Web in various sites.

One of the more popular products is Microsoft Project. A page devoted to it is found on the Microsoft Project Overview Page at *http://www.microsoft.com/products/ prodref/129_ov.htm*. Another site dealing with Microsoft Project is one grandly called "The Project Management World Wide Web Site" at *http:// www.projectmanagement.com/faqnew.htm*.

Another good project management software product is Scitor's Project Scheduler. A Web site for this product is at *http:// www.scitor.com/ps/ps7*. Demonstration versions of this product are available from these sites for free download.

BUSINESS NEWS

Every business manager needs to keep up with the business news. The Internet contains lots of good news sources, however, not everyone knows where to find it. Moreover, there are so many sources that nobody would have time to read them all, (even if they wanted to) and even searching them can be a major chore.

Everyone has different needs and interests regarding the news. The Net offers a way for people to customize their news, obtain it from all the major newspapers in the world and, in some cases, download it for future offline reading. One simple and effective way to do this is to select your favourite sources and bookmark them.

A good source of business news to bookmark would be "The Report on Business" of *The Globe and Mail* at *http://www.theglobeandmail.com*. Another good site containing general news as well as business news is the Canadian Canoe site

at *http://www.canoe.ca*. It contains a link to *The Financial Post* at *http://www.canoe.ca/FP/home.html*. For general as well as business news, the CBC has a news site at *http://www.cbc.ca*. Here, among other things, you can listen to live stereo radio broadcasts.

In the United States, *USA Today* has a site at *http://www.usatoday.com* and of course, at *http://www.cnn.com* there is the omniscient CNN, which has both business and financial news services. Both of these are good sources of current news.

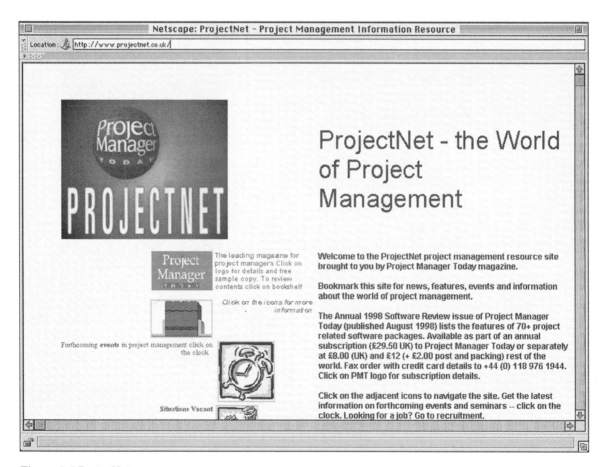

Figure 9.5 ProjectNet

Another new service of particular interest to business people is the Wall Street Journal Interactive Edition. Users subscribe to it for $49 per year, but it provides business from around the world. It's at *http://info.wsj.com*. A utility can be downloaded from the site called webex, which makes it possible to easily capture the news from this site and read it later.

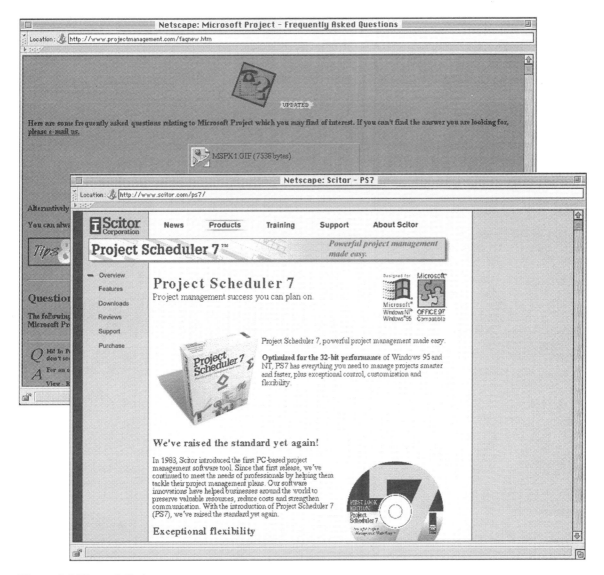

Figure 9.6 *Microsoft Project*
Figure 9.7 *Scitor's Project Scheduler*

Once you have located your preferred news sites, utilities can be downloaded and configured to automatically download your news of choice from the sites for later offline reading. These utilities work automatically when you log into the Net. A popular one is found at *http://www.pointcast.com*, which acts as a screen saver bannering the latest news headlines. CNN is offering a similar tool now, and there are many others. Many people feel that pointcasting, as opposed to broadcast-

ing, is the wave of the future, and the first step toward customized newspapers.

A little planning and set up time can save you a lot of time surfing the Net for news and can substantially improve your familiarity with the latest news events that could impact your business or that of your clients.

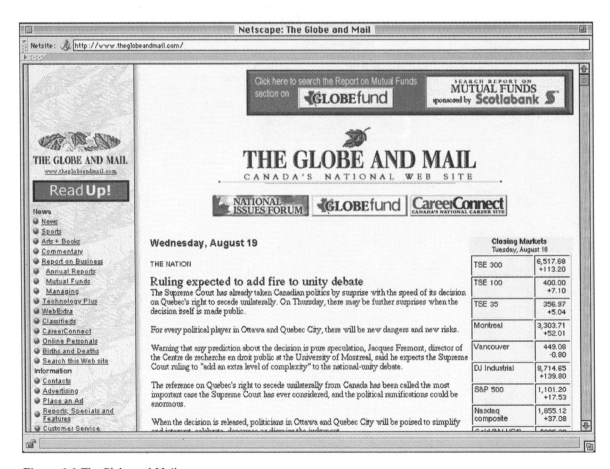

Figure 9.8 *The Globe and Mail*

MANAGEMENT RESEARCH

A Business Researcher's Interests at *http://www.brint.com/interest.html* is a searchable knowledge map of contemporary business, management and information technology issues. It provides access to hundreds of full-text articles and papers, magazines and journals, case studies and tools, and thousands of other resources on some of

Figure 9.9 USA Today
Figure 9.10 CNN Interactive

the hottest issues of interest to business, technology, and information professionals. Cutting-edge topics include business process reengineering, knowledge management, organizational learning, complex systems and chaos, intranets, virtual corporations, outsourcing, electronic markets, and electronic commerce. Also included

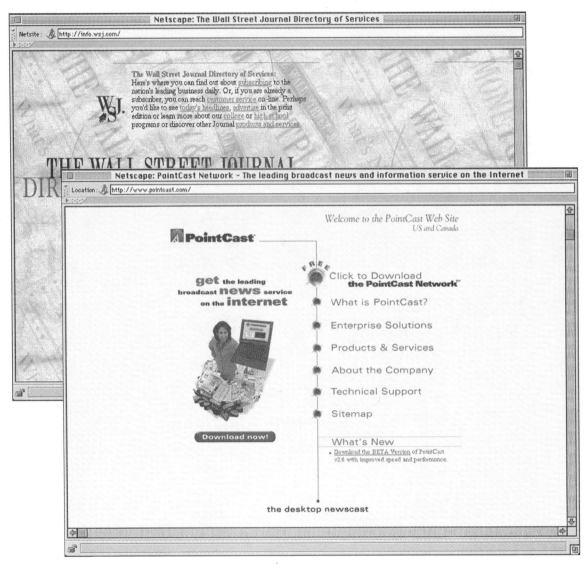

Figure 9.11 *Wall Street Journal*
Figure 9.12 *PointCast*

are a research jumpstation for all areas of business research, international business issues, intellectual property issues, information policy issues, Web strategy and marketing issues, and key applications of information systems research.

BRINT, with its impressive range of classified links, provides a powerful starting point for those interested in almost any aspect of business research.

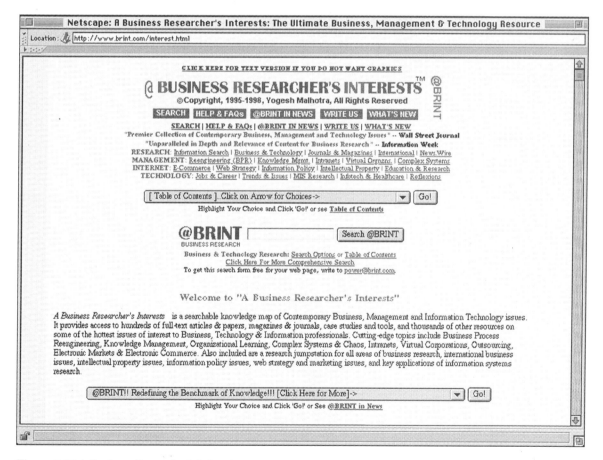

Figure 9.13 A Business Researcher's Interests

SUMMARY OF WEB SITES MENTIONED IN THIS CHAPTER

Name/Address

Harvard Business School
http//.www.hbs.edu

The Peter F. Drucker Foundation (US)
http://www.pfdf.org

The Peter F. Drucker Foundation (Can)
http://www.drucker.com

The Peter F. Drucker Graduate Management Center
http://www.cgsweb.cgs.edu/drucker/page_one.html

American Management Association (AMA) International
http://www.amanet.org

Canadian Management Centre (CMC)
http://www.cmcamai.org

Certified Management Consultants Association
http://www.cmc-consult.org

Center for International Project and Program Management (CIPPM)
http://ireland.iol.ie/~mattewar/CIPPM/

Project Management Institute
http://www.pmi.org

ProjectNet
http://www.projectnet.co.uk

Scitor Project Scheduler
http://www.scitor.com/ps/ps7

The Project Management World Wide Web Site
http://www.projectmanagement.com/faqnew.htm

Microsoft Project Overview Page
http://www.microsoft.com/products/prodref/129_ov.htm

The Globe and Mail "Report on Business"
http://www.theglobeandmail.com

Canadian Online Explorer (Canoe)
http://www.canoe.ca

The Financial Post
http://www.canoe.ca/FP/home.html

CBC
http://www.cbc.ca

USA Today
http://www.usatoday.com

CNN
http://www.cnn.com

Wall Street Journal
http://info.wsj.com

Pointcast News Utility
http://www.pointcast.com

A Business Researcher's Interests
http://www.brint.com/interest.html

10 EDUCATION

INTRODUCTION

Education is a very broad area, even within the confines of matters of interest to accountants. We are attempting to cover it not from the viewpoint of an educator, but rather the viewpoint of a practicing accountant or accounting student who is interested in determining the educational programs available to them either through the Internet or about which information is available on the Internet.

The programs available through the Internet or related resources are expanding, as the use of distance education on the Net grows. We therefore have a separate section of this chapter dedicated to distance education.

First we offer a summary of sites that can be used to access educational institutions in Canada and elsewhere. Many of these institutions offer programs in accounting or related subjects and details can usually be found by going to their site and working through their menu systems to the business, business administration, management or accounting departments. In the previous chapter, we have mentioned several sites for graduate schools of management.

UNIVERSITIES

A good linked list of sites for Canadian universities is found at *http://*

www.uwaterloo.ca/canu/index.html. A similar list for universities in the United States can be found at www.clas.ufl.edu/CLAS/american-universities.html. In the United Kingdom, a map-based set of links is available at the Web site of the University of Wolverhampton at *http://www.scit.wlv.ac.uk/ukinfo/uk.map.html*.

COMMUNITY COLLEGES

Many accounting and business related subjects are taught at the so-called community colleges across the country. The term "community colleges" encompasses a wide variety of institution, including technology institutes and schools, specialized community schools, and colleges that are essentially similar to universities.

The Association of Canadian Community Colleges (ACCC) at *http://www.accc.ca/eng/about* has members that comprise all types of college. Their members focus on training needs of business, industry, the public service sectors and the educational needs of vocationally oriented secondary school graduates.

The Web site provides detailed information about the association, an excellent list of educational links at *http://www.accc.ca/eng/sites* and links to the Web sites of member institutions across the country.

SCHOOLS

Schools, in particular high schools, offer accounting and other business related courses and programs. Probably the most comprehensive of links to Canadian schools on the Web is found at *web66.coled.umn.edu/schools/CA/Canada.html*.

The use of technology in the classroom is gaining increasing attention. A good network for plugging into what is happening in various schools across the country in this area is SchoolNet. This Web site can be found at *http://www.schoolnet.ca/info* with the french version at *http://www.rescol.ca*. The goal of SchoolNet is to help to "facilitate excellence in learning through electronic networking across Canada". Many online resources are available on this Web site.

Such techniques, of course, are not limited to schools. Another site that offers much help in this area is the Computers

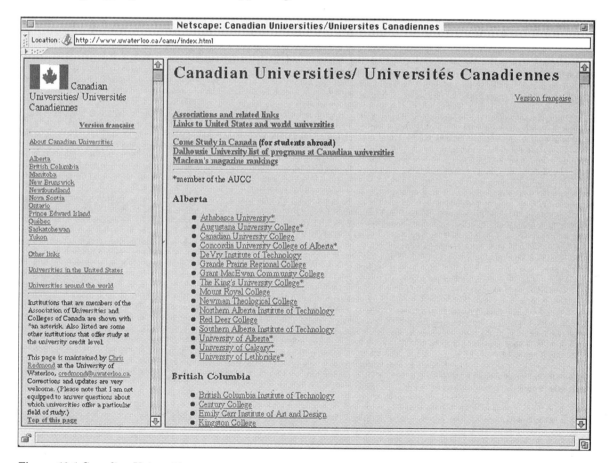

Figure 10.1 *Canadian Universities*

in Teaching Initiative at *info.ox.ac.uk/cti/index.html.*

DISTANCE EDUCATION

Many of the educational sites mentioned so far have somewhere within them references to distance education. However, since the Internet is growing as a vehicle for the delivery of distance education, we will report on many sites that are either exclusively devoted to this topic or have unusually extensive offerings in this area.

Established in 1983, the Canadian Association for Distance Education (CADE) is a national association devoted to the advancement of distance education in Canada. This association has a Web site at *http://www.cade-aced.ca.*

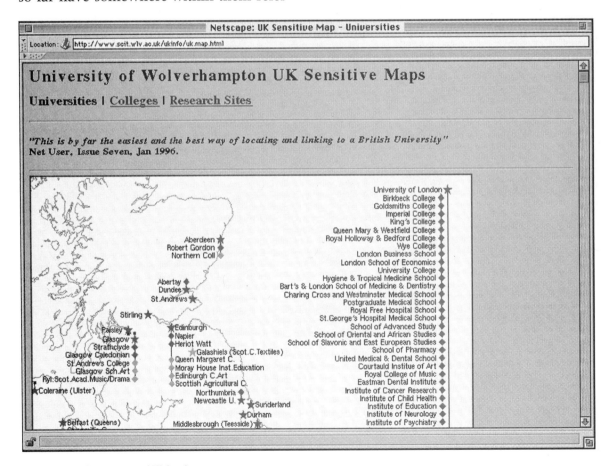

Figure 10.2 *University of Wolverhampton*

It covers material on the aims and objectives of the association, its various programs and services, information on its conferences, some of which are held in a distance format, and information about its magazine *Communique*.

It also publishes the *Journal of Distance Education*, a refereed journal which is published twice yearly. It serves as a forum to reflect current theory, research and practice related to teaching and learning at a distance.

Among particular institutions offering programs through distance education, one that deserves a particular mention is Athabasca University at *http://www.athabascau.ca*.

Athabasca offers probably one of the more extensive distance learning programs in Canada. Their program includes an MBA degree, which can be obtained over two to three years, on the Internet, except for a required summer school and two other

Figure 10.3 *Association of Canadian Community Colleges*

short in-house sessions. Other Bachelor of Administration programs are offered.

Several other universities offer Internet based programs. IS World Net Page for IS Education (Courses) at *http://*

www.cba.bgsu.edu / amis / smagal / isedu (parts of it are under development) attempts to offer information about courses available in the area of Information Systems.

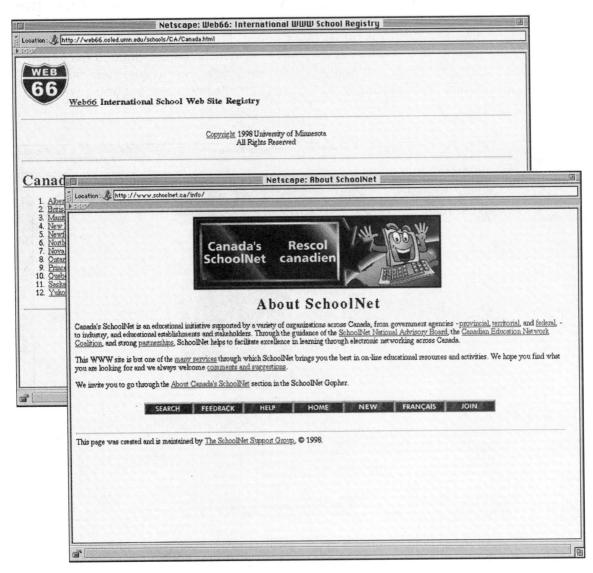

Figure 10.4 Web66
Figure 10.5 SchoolNet

The University of Waterloo has several distance education programs, some in the field of business, which are described at *http://www.adm.uwaterloo.ca/infoded/de&ce.html*. As stated there, "Distance Education, a convenient alternative to attending classes, enables students to complete all the requirements for a UW degree in Arts, Science, and Environmental Studies.

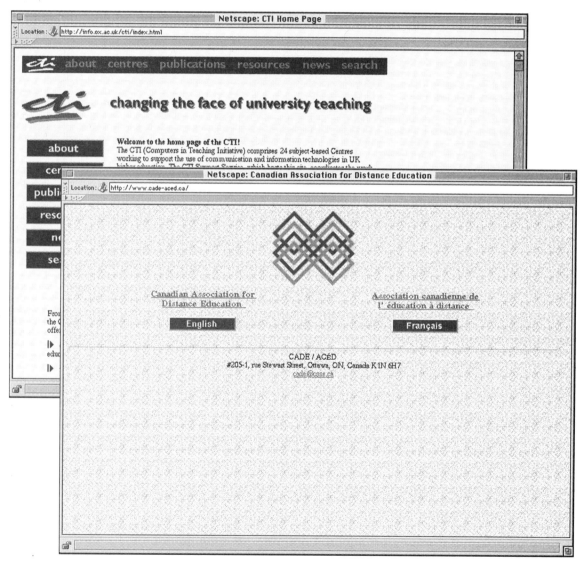

Figure 10.6 CTI Computers in Teaching Initiative
Figure 10.7 Canadian Association for Distance Education

Over 250 degree credit undergraduate courses are available".

Another prominent institution that offers distance education programs is Simon Fraser University, with a Web site at *http://*

www.sfu.ca/cde. Through its Centre for Distance Education, Simon Fraser offers one of the largest distance education programs in Canada, with approximately "12,000 course enrolments a year in 118 credit

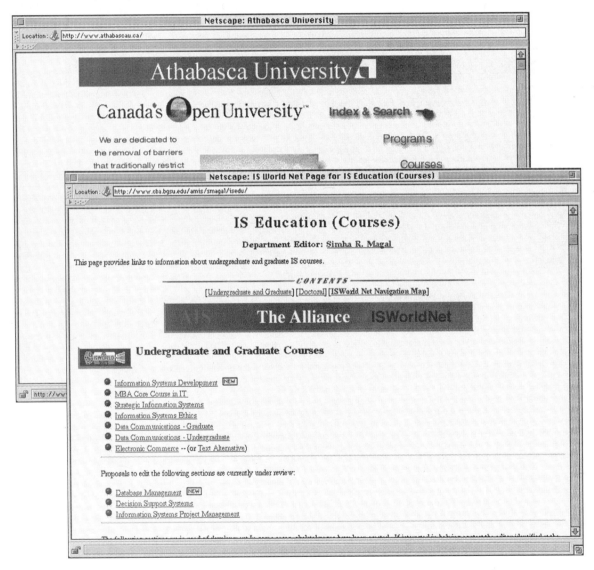

Figure 10.8 *Athabasca University*
Figure 10.9 *IS Education*

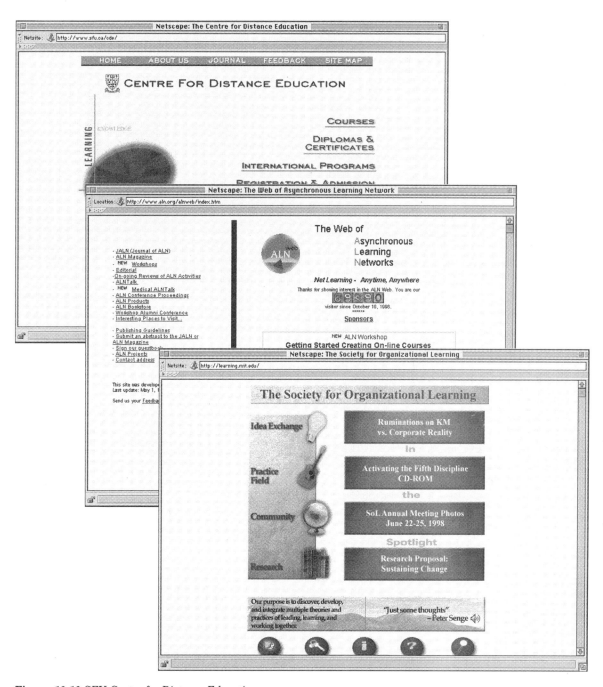

Figure 10.10 *SFU Centre for Distance Education*
Figure 10.11 *Asynchronous Learning Network*
Figure 10.12 *Massachusetts Institute of Technology*

courses". Formal academic programs include degrees, certificates, or post-baccalaureate diplomas in a number of fields.

A tremendous source of information about advanced learning techniques in a virtual educational environment is the site of the Asychronous Learning Network (ALN) at *http://www.aln.org/alnweb/index/htm.* This exhaustive site offers many articles, the *ALN Magazine,* the *Journal of ALN,* a good list of site links, and details about conferences and workshops. The site provides insights into the concept of the virtual university that are well worth considering. The site contains reports on two virtual universities, Diversity University and Athena University.

Education is increasingly being linked to on-the-job training, in recognition that many jobs in our technological world are constantly changing and that employees need constant training in a learning environment. Also there is a need for linkage programs that build on the prior educational experience of workers to enable them to function more productively in the work environment.

The Massachusetts Institute of Technology has established the MIT Organizational Learning Network at *learning.mit.edu* in recognition of these needs. The site provides a wealth of information about the characteristics of learning organizations. It also offers a forum for exchange of ideas, detailed case studies and sound research reports on the topic. It is one of the better sites dealing with organizational learning on the Web.

For those who are interested in developing Web based courses, an interesting site is at *ibt.testprep.com.* Called the IBTpublisher Home Page, the site features authoring software to enable the production of such courses. Online demos and other details are offered in the site.

Another site specifically directed to accountants is that of The Internet Learning Centre, located at *http://www.netlearn.ca.* This site is under development at the time of writing, but proposes to offer online pre- and post-qualification courses to professional accountants.

Finally numerous links to Web sites dealing with distance education are found on Yahoo! at *http://www.yahoo.ca/Education/Distance_Learning.*

SUMMARY OF WEB SITES MENTIONED IN THIS CHAPTER

Name/Address

Canadian Universities
http://www.uwaterloo.ca/canu/index.html

American Universities
http://www.clas.ufl.edu/CLAS/american-universities.html

UK Sensitive Map – Academic
http://www.scit.wlv.ac.uk/ukinfo/uk.map.html

Association of Canadian Community Colleges
http://www.accc.ca/eng/about

Association of Canadian Community Colleges – Links
http://www.accc.ca/eng/sites

Canadian Schools on the WWW
http://web66.coled.umn.edu/schools/CA/Canada.html

SchoolNet
http://www.schoolnet.ca/info/http://www.rescol.ca

Computers in Teaching Initiative
http://info.ox.ac.uk/cti/index.html

Canadian Association of Distance Education
http://www.cadee-aced.ca

Athabasca University
http://www.athabascau.ca

IS World Net Page for IS Education (Courses)
http://www.cba.bgsu.edu/amis/smagal/isedu

University of Waterloo
http://www.adm.uwaterloo.ca/infoded/de&ce.html

Simon Fraser University
http://www.sfu.ca/cde

Asychronous Learning Network
http://www.aln.org/alnweb/index/htm

The MIT Organizational Learning Network
http://learning.mit.edu

The IBTpublisher Home Page
http://ibt.testprep.com

Internet Learning Centre
http://www.netlearn.ca

Yahoo! Distance Education Sites
http://www.yahoo.ca/Education/Distance_Learning

11 REGULATORY AUTHORITIES, TRADE, AND CURRENCY INFORMATION

INTRODUCTION

SECURITIES COMMISSIONS

ACCOUNTING
PROFESSIONAL PRACTICE AND STANDARDS

BUSINESS ASSOCIATIONS AND REGULATORY SITES

GOVERNMENT ORGANIZATIONS AND ASSOCIATIONS

CURRENCY INFORMATION

SUMMARY OF WEB SITES MENTIONED IN CHAPTER 11

INTRODUCTION

As the Internet continues to grow, so does the number of sites containing information that regulates the way companies do business in Canada. These include, but are not limited to, the various exchange commissions for capital stock issuance and reporting of financial results, institutes and associations that govern their members' practices, taxation authorities, and other authorities that regulate the way an organization can do business (such as the CRTC). This chapter discusses a number of those that are now online. It also discusses the availability of up-to-date currency information and currency converters that are available to assist an accountant in doing calculations involving foreign exchange.

SECURITIES COMMISSIONS

This chapter does not discuss the Securities Commissions in any detail as they are addressed fully in next chapter, Securities Information.

ACCOUNTING

PROFESSIONAL PRACTICE AND STANDARDS

There are a number of types of professional accountants in Canada that have professional institutes that govern their practice. Chartered accountants are governed by both a national and a provincial institute. The Canadian Institute of Chartered Accountants at *http://www.cica.ca* has been mentioned numerous times throughout this book. Provincial organizations also guide a chartered accountant. Membership and practice determine which provincial or territorial association is applicable. The list of provincial and territorial sites, along with their Internet addresses, are as follows:

- The Institute of Chartered Accountants of Alberta at *http://www.icaa.ab.ca*

- The Institute of Chartered Accountants of British Columbia at *http://www.ica.bc.ca/*

- The Institute of Chartered Accountants of Manitoba at *http://www.icam.mb.ca/*

- The New Brunswick Institute of Chartered Accountants at *http://www.nbica.org/*

- The Institute of Chartered Accountants of Nova Scotia at *http://www.icans.ns.ca/*

- The Institute of Chartered Accountants of Ontario at *http://www.icao.on.ca*

- Ordre des comptables agréés du Québec at *http://www.ocaq.qc.ca*

• The Institute of Chartered Accountants of Saskatchewan at *http://www.icas.sk.ca*, although the site requires a user name and password for entry.

These sites can be accessed directly from the CICA home site. Other provincial or territorial associations not listed above do not currently have a site.

There are other accounting bodies that have their professional institutes online. The Certified General Accountants' Association of Canada at *http://www.cga-canada.org*. They also have a page of links to their provincial assocations at their site. Their provincial organizations having WWW links are:

• Certified General Accountants Association of Alberta at *http://www.cga-alberta.org*

• Certified General Accountants Association of British Columbia at *http://www.cga-bc.org*

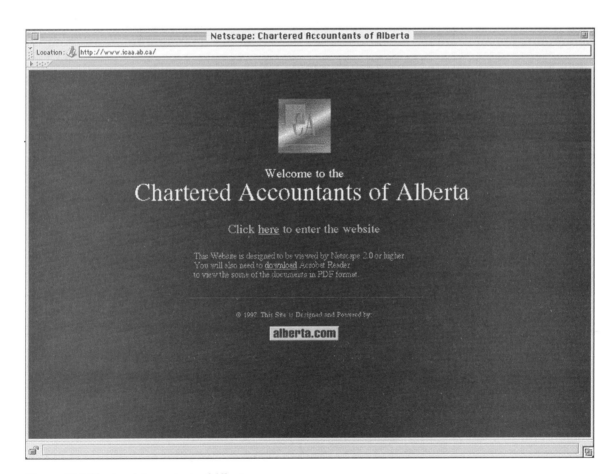

Figure 11.1 Chartered Accountants of Alberta

- Certified General Accountants Association of Manitoba at *http://www.cga-manitoba.org/*

- Certified General Accountants Association of New Brunswick at *http://www.cga-nb.org/*

- Certified General Accountants Association of Newfoundland at *http://www.cabot.nf.ca*

- Certified General Accountants Association of North West Territories is at *http://www.cga-nwt.org*

- Certified General Accountants Association of Nova Scotia (from Dalhousie) at *http://www.cga-ns.org*, although it is in progress

- Certified General Accountants Association of Ontario at *http://cga-ontario.org*

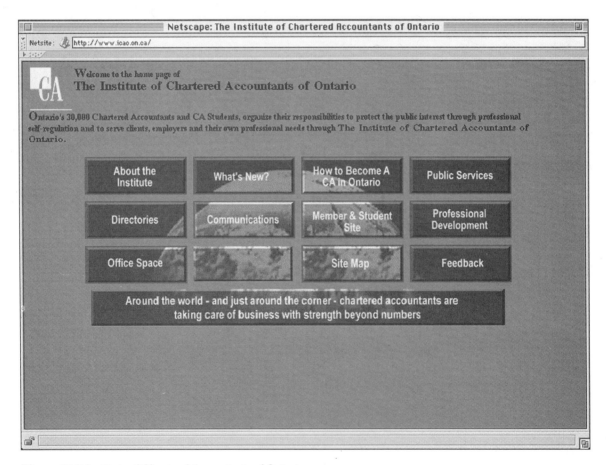

Figure 11.2 *Institute of Chartered Accountants of Ontario*

- Certified General Accountants Association of Prince Edward Island at *http://www.cga-pei.org/*

- Certified General Accountants Association of Québec at *http://cga-quebec.org*

- Certified General Accountants Association of Saskatchewan at *http://www.cga-canada.org/saskatchewan/index.htm*

The links above are best accessed through the CGA Canada site.

The final major accounting association in Canada is The Society of Management Accountants of Canada at *http://www.cma-canada.org/english/cma1.html*. It also has a provincial link page that should be used for easier access. Its provincial organizations that currently have sites are:

- Certified Management Accountants Society of British Columbia at *http://www.cmabc.com/*

- The Society of Management Accountants of Alberta at *http://www.cmaab.com/*

- The Society of Management Accountants of Manitoba at *http://www.cma-canada.org/SMAM/home.html*

- The Society of Management Accountants of Ontario at *http://www.cma-ontario.org/*

- Ordre des comptables en management accrédités du Québec at *http://www.cma-quebec.org/index2.html*

- The Society of Management Accountants (Maritime Office) at *http://www.purdyswharf.com/CMA/*

Another accounting group that can be found on the WWW is The Petroleum Accountants Society of Canada at *http://www.cadvision.com/pasc/*. This organization promotes standards and information in oil and gas accounting.

BUSINESS ASSOCIATIONS AND REGULATORY SITES

There are hundreds of business organizations in Canada. Perhaps the most comprehensive information on associations, government, etc. is still in paper and CD-ROM format only. The Canadian Almanac & Directory (CAD), as most librarians will attest, is one of the most valuable reference tools in any type of library's collection. The CAD provides statistical and background information in areas such as arts and culture, business and finance, industry, labour, government and public administration, geography, communications, education, transportation, science and technology, society, health and medicine, and the legal and judicial system and has over 200,000 records. There is no Internet version available for this yet.

To ascertain whether an organization has a site, one can either use a search engine with the name as the search criteria or use a 411 service. The following is a list of some of the various associations and their sites. This list concentrates mainly on accounting, finance and business associations.

- Bank of Canada at *http://www.bank-banque-canada.ca/* does not carry out ordinary banking business, nor does it accept deposits from the general public; however it does influence the economic circumstances of businesses and individuals across the country.

- The Canadian Association of Financial Planners at *http://www.cafp.org/* is the

organization that governs certified financial planners. The site contains rules and regulations, ethics, how to find a planner, etc.

- Canadian Exporters' Association at *http://www.palantir.ca/the-alliance/* brings together manufacturers, trading houses, consulting engineers, contractors, legal firms, consultants, financial institutions, and companies providing services to exporters.

Figure 11.3 Society of Management Accountants of Canada

- The Canadian Association of Home Inspectors at *http://www.telusplanet.net/public/moemad/cahi2.html* is the "umbrella group" under which all the Canadian chapters operate. The CAHI® undertakes to negotiate and mediate any issues that need to be dealt with on a national rather than a regional level.

- Since 1971, the Canadian Federation of Independent Business at *http://www.cfib.ca/* has been giving small firms a big voice in the public arena.

- Canadian Economics Association (CEA) at *http://economics.ca/* with approximately 1000 members across the country and from abroad is the organization of academic economists in Canada.

- Canadian Finance & Leasing Association at *http://www.cfla-acfl.ca/* is the nonprofit association that represents the interests of the asset-based financing, equipment, and vehicle leasing industry in Canada.

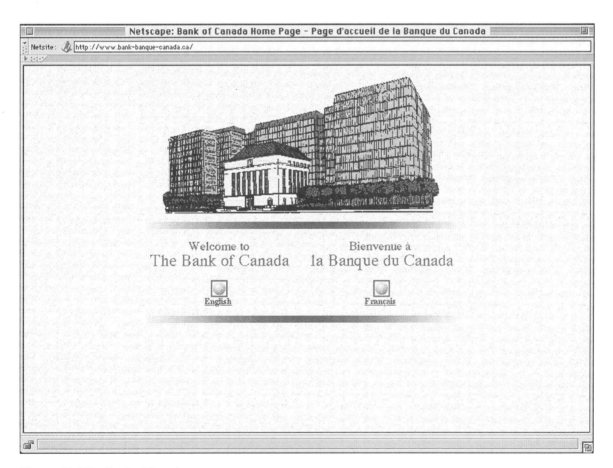

Figure 11.4 The Bank of Canada

- Canadian Home Builders Association at *http://www.chba.ca* is the voice of the residential construction industry in Canada.

- Canadian Venture Capital Association at *http://www.cvca.ca/* was founded in July 1974 to represent the interests of its members by promoting the development

Figure 11.5 *Canadian Economics Association*
Figure 11.6 *Financial Executives Institute Canada*

and advancement of Canadian business enterprises through the use of venture capital, and promoting and fostering professional development, communication, and association among all corporations, companies, partnerships, syndicates, and persons engaged in venture capital investments in Canada.

- Financial Executives Institute Canada at *http://www.fei.org* with 11 chapters, is part of a 91-chapter North American organization that boasts 14,000 members from more than 8,000 corporations throughout Canada and the United States.

- Insurance Bureau of Canada at *http://www.ibc.ca* represents companies that insure the homes, cars, and businesses of Canadians.

- Industry Network Canada Inc. (Incan) at *http://www.incan.com* profiles Canadian companies, coast to coast, with the intent to promote and support these companies around the world (making a spot on the site ideal for Canadian exporters).

- Treasury Management Association of Canada at *http://www.tmac.ca/* is a federation of 16 regional associations of professional treasury managers. TMAC members are responsible for treasury functions in the multi-billion dollar Canadian market-place.

As mentioned above, this is just an illustration of the vast number of trade, business, and other associations available in Canada. Remember to use a detailed search to get the fastest link to the particular association you want.

GOVERNMENT ORGANIZATIONS AND ASSOCIATIONS

Most of the discussion on government and government sites was set out in Chapter 7 and will not, for the most part, be repeated. For accountants, certainly, the most important site is the Department of Finance Canada at *http://www.fin.gc.ca*. The Department of Finance Canada is primarily responsible for providing the Government of Canada with analysis and advice on the broad economic and financial affairs of Canada.

Another good link of the Government of Canada site that should be kept in mind is at *http://canada.gc.ca/depts/major/depind_e.html*. This provides a fully linked index to all federal organizations. It has in excess of 100 links and should be viewed as a primary bookmark to federal organizations. The sites it currently accesses include (please note that since the site is fully indexed the individual department's URLs have not been listed):

- Bank of Canada

- Business Development Bank of Canada

- Canada Deposit Insurance Corporation
- Canada Labour Relations Board
- Canada Mortgage and Housing Corporation
- Canadian Environmental Assessment Agency
- Canadian Film Development Corporation
- Canadian Human Rights Commission
- Canadian International Development Agency
- Canadian International Trade Tribunal
- Canadian Radio-Television and Telecommunications Commission
- Communications Security Establishment
- Export Development Corporation
- Farm Credit Corporation Canada
- Department of Finance Canada

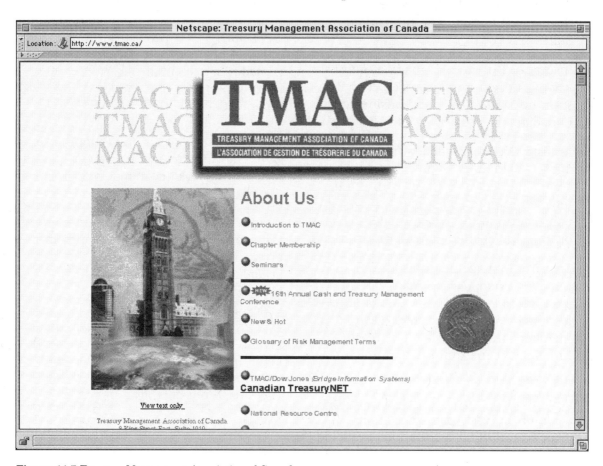

Figure 11.7 *Treasury Management Association of Canada*

- Canada Investment and Savings

- Health Canada

- Human Resources Development Canada

- Industry Canada

- Canadian Intellectual Property Office

- National Round Table on the Environment and the Economy

- Office of the Auditor General of Canada

- Office of the Superintendent of Financial Institutions Canada

- Prime Minister's Office

- Consulting and Audit Canada

- Receiver General for Canada

- Revenue Canada

- Standards Council of Canada

- Statistics Canada

- Treasury Board of Canada Secretariat

- Western Economic Diversification Canada

CURRENCY INFORMATION

Most organizations exist in a global marketplace and, within that marketplace, there exists a multitude of currencies that have to be dealt with. Fortunately there are a number of sites that are available to assist the accountant in obtaining up-to-date currency information to facilitate international analysis or to do foreign exchange accounting.

First of all, there are the bank sites that were discussed in Chapter 6. Many have exchange rate data available at their sites. If you are looking at more comprehensive information then you should do a search using the search string "currency converters". Many sites are available, but three of our favourites are:

- Universal Currency Converter by Xenon Labratories at *http://www.xe.net/currency/* allows you to perform interactive foreign exchange rate conversion on the Internet. You need to type the amount of source currency in the input box. You select the source and destination currencies using the scrolling selection. When you are finished, you click the "Perform Currency Conversion" button, and the results of your conversion will be displayed.

- Exchange Rates at *http://www.dna.lth.se/cgi-bin//kurt/* rates uses rates provided by the Federal Reserve Bank of New York at approximately noon (EST) on the given date. This table provides currency comparisons between 37 currencies:

  –Australian Dollar

  –Austrian Schilling

  –Belgian Franc

  –Brazilian Real

–British Pound

–Canadian Dollar

–Chinese (P.R.) Yuan

–Danish Krone

–Dutch Guilder

–European Union Euro

–Finnish Markka

–French Franc

–German Mark

–Greek Drachma

–Hong Kong Dollar

–Indian Rupee

–Irish Pound

–Israeli Shekel

–Italian Lira

–Japanese Yen

–Malaysian Ringgit

–Mexican Peso

–New Zealand Dollar

–Norwegian Krone

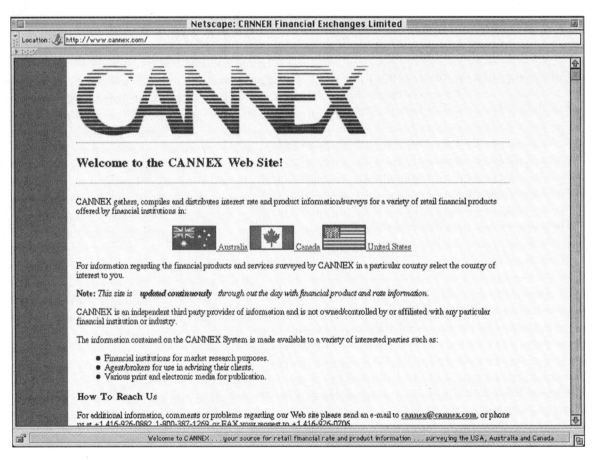

Figure 11.8 CANNEX

–Philippines Pesos

–Portuguese Escudo

–Singapore Dollar

–South African Rand

–South Korean Won

–Spanish Peseta

–Sri Lankan Rupee

–Swedish Krona

–Swiss Franc

–Taiwan N.T. Dollar

–Thai Baht

–United States Dollar

–Venezuelan Bolivar

• CANNEX at *http://www.cannex.com/* provides near real-time interest rate information for a variety of Australian, Canadian and US financial products. The site is updated continuously throughout the day with financial product and rate information.

As mentioned above, there are a number of sites that have currency conversion information (over 12,000 according to AltaVista). It is important to experiment and choose the one which might prove the most useful. But don't waste too much time finding it.

SUMMARY OF WEB SITES MENTIONED IN THIS CHAPTER

Name/Address

The Canadian Institute of Chartered Accountants
http://www.cica.ca

The Institute of Chartered Accountants of Alberta
http://www.icaa.ab.ca

The Institute of Chartered Accountants of British Columbia
http://www.ica.bc.ca/

The Institute of Chartered Accountants of Manitoba
http://www.icam.mb.ca

The New Brunswick Institute of Chartered Accountants
http://www.nbica.org

The Institute of Chartered Accountants of Nova Scotia
http://www.icans.ns.ca

The Institute of Chartered Accountants of Ontario
http://www.icao.on.ca

Ordre des comptables agréés du Québec
http://www.ocaq.qc.ca

The Institute of Chartered Accountants of Saskatchewan
http://www.icas.sk.ca

The Certified General Accountants Association of Canada
http://www.cga-canada.org

Certified General Accountants Association of Alberta
http://www.cga-alberta.org

Certified General Accountants Association of British Columbia
http://www.cga-bc.org

Certified General Accountants Association of Manitoba
http://www.cga-manitoba.org

Certified General Accountants Association of New Brunswick
http://www.cga-nb.org/

Certified General Accountants Association of Newfoundland
http://www. cabot.nf.ca

Certified General Accountants Association of North West Territories
http://www.cga-nwt.org

Certified General Accountants Association of Nova Scotia (from Dalhousie)
http://www. cga-ns.org

Certified General Accountants Association of Ontario
http://cga-ontario.org

Certified General Accountants Association of Prince Edward Island
http://www.cga-pei.org

Certified General Accountants Association of Québec
http://cga-quebec.org

The Society of Management Accountants of Canada
http://www.cma-canada.org/english/cma1.html

Certified Management Accountants Society of British Columbia
http://www.cmabc.com/

The Society of Management Accountants of Alberta
http://www.cmaab.com/

The Society of Management Accountants of Manitoba
http://www.cma-canada.org/SMAM/home.html

The Society of Management Accountants of Ontario
http://www.cma-ontario.org/

Ordre des comptables en management accrédités du Québec
http://www.cma-quebec.org/index2.html

The Society of Management Accountants (Maritime Office)
http://www.purdyswharf.com/CMA/

The Petroleum Accountants Society of Canada
http://www.cadvision.com/pasc/

Bank of Canada
http://www.bank-banque-canada.ca/

The Canadian Association of Financial Planners
http://www.cafp.org/

Canadian Exporters' Association
http://www.palantir.ca/the-alliance/

The Canadian Association of Home Inspectors
http://www.telusplanet.net/public/moemad/cahi2.html

Canadian Federation of Independent Business
http://www.cfib.ca/

Canadian Economics Association
http://economics.ca/

Canadian Finance & Leasing Association
http://www.cfla-acfl.ca/

Canadian Home Builders Association
http://www.cvca.ca/

Financial Executives Institute Canada
http://www.fei.org

Insurance Bureau of Canada
http://www.ibc.ca

Industry Network Canada Inc.
http://www.incan.com

Treasury Management Association of Canada
http://www.tmac.ca/

Department of Finance Canada
http://www.fin.gc.ca

Government of Canada (index)
http://canada.gc.ca/depts/major/depind_e.html

Universal Currency Converter by Xenon Labratories
http://www.xe.net/currency/

Exchange Rates
http://www.dna.lth.se/cgi-bin//kurt/rates

CANNEX
http://www.cannex.com/

12 SECURITIES INFORMATION

INTRODUCTION

There are two aspects of securities that usually interest accountants. The first, and most common, is investment in securities. Here, their interest is similar to that of many other people in society, but their orientation is different. Accountants tend to be relatively sophisticated about the presentation and analysis of financial information, therefore their interests in information needed to make investment decisions tend to include a greater emphasis on the analysis of available financial information.

The other, more specialized, interest of accountants in securities is that of those who practice in the securities field. This might include public accountants who provide assurance services with respect to prospectuses, general practitioners who offer advice to companies going public, and accountants who work within the regulatory agencies. There is considerable information about both aspects of securities on the Web. We will attempt to identify the more useful and complete sites.

Investing in securities involves two distinct stages:

1. deciding what to buy initially, and

2. monitoring progress on some periodic basis in order to decide whether to sell or hold the investment.

INVESTMENT RESEARCH

The Web offers unique opportunities to research potential investments, since there is not only information about stock market prices and experience, but also extensive information about particular companies that represent investment opportunities on their own Web sites.

Probably the best place to find links of interest to Canadian investors is the Canadian Financial Network Inc. at *http://www.canadianfinance.com*. This wide-ranging site contains numerous links to sites in several relevant categories, including lists of accountants, advisors, banks, brokers, news commentary, futures and options, investment research, mutual funds, real estate and insurance, venture capital, and international financial links. Many of the remaining sites mentioned in this chapter were garnered from these links.

In deciding how to choose investments, it is important to gain an understanding of the current economic and investment environment. Several sites are available on the Web to offer helpful information, including the Government of Canada sites mentioned in earlier chapters, and particularly the Statistics Canada and Department of Finance sites and the Bank of Canada site at *http://www.bank-banque-canada.ca*. The Bank of Canada site offers access to its publications, current market rates, weekly financial statistics, and information on Canada Savings Bonds, Canadian currency, and other material.

Another good government agency site is that of Canada Investment and Savings at *http://www.cis-pec.gc.ca*. This site provides a wealth of information about Canada Savings Bonds and other investments. The stated goal of the organization is "to provide individual Canadians better access to existing Government of Canada securities, such as Canada Savings Bonds, Treasury Bills and marketable bonds, and to develop new investment products to help them meet their savings and investment needs".

News sites on the World Wide Web are plentiful. However, as with most information on the Web, the most relevant and useful information for a particular purpose is often difficult to find amidst the plethora. The mainstream press, such as *The Globe and Mail* and *The Financial Post*, have good Web sites as mentioned in Chapter 9.

A good source of financial news is Canadian Corporate News at *http://www.cdn-news.com*. It publishes press re-

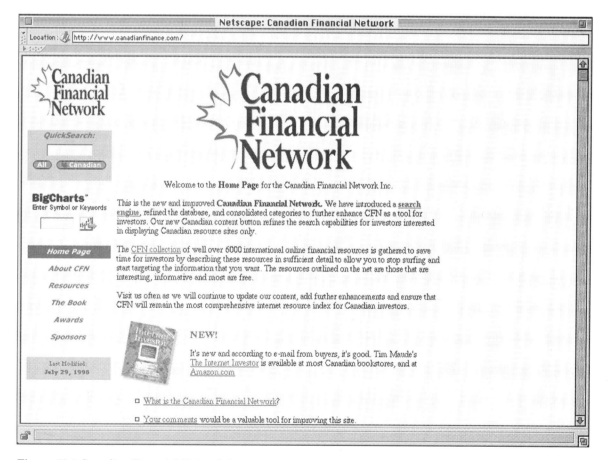

Figure 12.1 Canadian Financial Network Inc.

leases of Canadian public corporations and is a great early source of news being released by those corporations.

Infoglobe at *qsilver.queensu.ca / law / infoglob.htm* provides access to "full text, reference, financial / stock market, and other databases (federal and Ontario budgets, Dynis Canadian Trademarks)". It is a vehicle of the Thomson chain of companies, and therefore offers access to *The Globe and Mail* as well as other news vehicles.

If access to these newsy web sites does not satisfy particular investment needs, then it is possible to subscribe to an email list for investment analysis purposes. One of these is called "Bidding on Bay Street" at *http://www.eucanect.com/investments/bayst.html*. This service provides frequent updates on Canadian companies through email *BAY $TREET BYTE$*. Instructions are on the Web site.

There are many facets to investment research. For those with a leaning to gold

Figure 12.2 Canadian Corporate News

stocks, the Gold Mining Stock Report at *http://www.infomine.com/newsletters/websites/gmsr.html* is available monthly for a fee.

A newsletter devoted to a range of mining issues can be obtained from the Hard Rock Analyst at *http://www.info-mine.com/hra*.

Some investors prefer investing in the complex area of commodity futures. The Winnipeg Commodities Exchange has a Web site at *http://www.wce.mb.ca* which provides information about such commodities as wheat, canola, flaxseed and barley.

Market quotes from the Winnipeg Commodities Exchange are available at *http://www.telenium.ca/WCE*.

Some more general but useful reference sources are found at the Internet Financial Connection *http://www.ifcstocks.com* and Investors Guru at *home.istar.ca/~invguru*. The Investors Newsletter Digest at *http://*

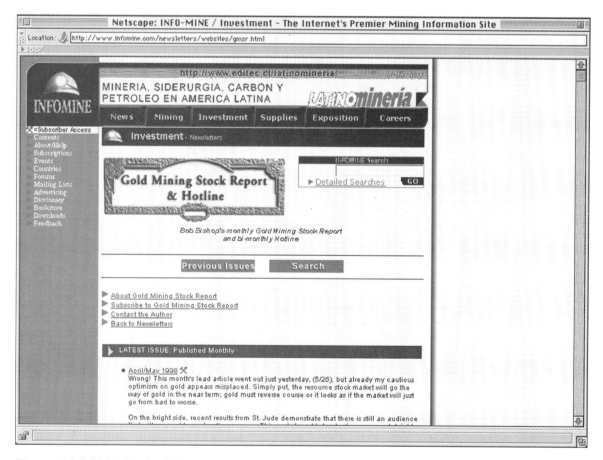

Figure 12.3 *Gold Mining Stock Report*

www.investorsnews.com and The Canadian Stock Market Reporter at *http://www.canstock.com* provide useful information on potential buys and sells.

Investing in mutual funds has, of course, shown tremendous growth in recent years, spurred largely by the increase in the use of registered retirement funds. As mentioned in Chapter 6, information about the mutual funds of the banks is available at the bank sites.

However, there are other sources as well. An advisory letter for Canadian mutual funds, The Fund Counsel, can be found at *http://www.fundcounsel.com*. This publication, available for a subscription fee, provides timely information about the Canadian investment scene.

The Business Development Bank of Canada at *http://www.bdc.ca* delivers timely and relevant financial and management services, with a particular focus on the

Figure 12.4 *Winnipeg Commodities Exchange*

emerging and exporting sectors of the economy.

MONITORING INVESTMENTS

Watching investments, as mentioned above, is a necessary part of the investment decision process—the decision to hold or sell. Stock Quotes on the North American exchanges can be found at Telequote, which has a Web site at *http://www.telequote.com*.

CBS MarketWatch at *mw.dbc.com* touts itself as "America's leading provider of real-time market data to the individual Investor". It offers quotes for the New York and American Stock Exchanges, NASDAQ, and other data, including Canadian, for a fee of $29.95 per month.

Figure 12.5 The Fund Counsel

The Canada Net Financial Pages at *http://www.cyberion.com/canadanet* also provides stock quotes from the TSE, VSE, MSE and ASE, and Canadian mutual funds. In addition, it provides searchable databases of articles and analysis from the Canadian Society of Technical Analysis at *http://www.csta.org*.

If you are interested in investing in a business or real estate development, check out The Investment Exchange at *http://www.worldweb.com/ubs*. It has an international data base of thousands of entrepreneurs and investors.

There are numerous useful real estate sites, many of them focusing on a particular city or region.

The Canadian Home Builders Association has a Web site at *http://www.chba.ca* which features useful information on buying a new home. In addition, the Canadian Association of Home inspectors at *http://www.bconnex.net/~jmlueck/cahi.html* provides links to several real estate industry related sites.

Some sites providing interest rate information were mentioned above. However, one that offers more information related to interest rates in the real estate industry is the site of CANNEX at *http://www.cannex.com*. It provides interest rate information for a variety of Canadian and US financial products.

There is also the site of the Canadian Mortgage and Housing Corporation at *http://www.cmhc-schl.gc.ca/cmhc.html*. CMHC is characterized as "Canada's most

comprehensive source of information on housing, whether you're a home owner, a potential buyer, a renovator, or a builder, or if you have special housing needs".

Keeping track of and analyzing investments can be made easier with useful financial software. Several money management products, such as Microsoft Money, offer capabilities in this area. However, a more specialized capability is found at *http://www.chartsmart.com*. The CHARTSMART software package covers most stocks on the VSE, ASE, and TSE.

SECURITIES REGULATION

Information about securities regulation is of considerable interest to practicing accountants who provide services in this complex field, such as prospectus work and assistance with going public. It is also of interest to accountants who are working within a company that is either public or going public.

The World Wide Web contains some very relevant information on the regulation of securities and a good deal more is expected in the next several months. The primary sources of this information are the regulatory agencies—the provincial securities commissions and the stock exchanges. But there are other private sites that also offer useful information and that are quickly becoming regular reference sources for those involved in this challenging field.

The acknowledged leader in securities regulation in Canada, the Ontario Securities Commission, has a site at *http:// www.osc.gov.on.ca/*. This is an excellent site with extensive detailed information about the OSC and its rules and regulations. It also includes details of recent rulings and hearings and a complete list of all registrants and reporting issuers, including links to SEDAR. The site includes links to other major regulators in Canada and around the world. The OSC site is of major importance to Canadian investors and securities-related accounting practitioners.

Another relatively new site is that of the Toronto Stock Exchange at *http:// www.tse.com*. Also an extremely informative site, the TSE has considerable information to help investors and securities practitioners.

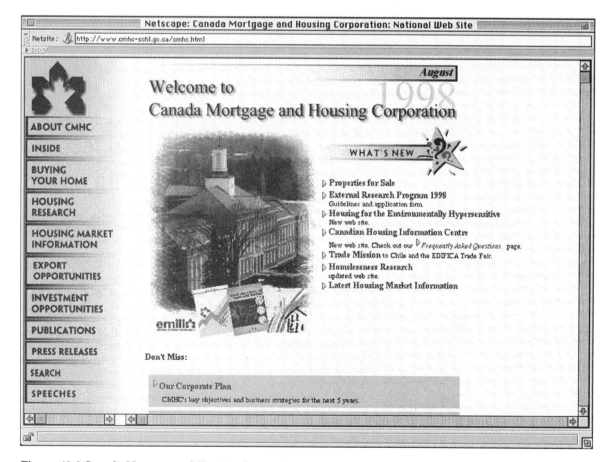

Figure 12.6 Canada Mortgage and Housing Corporation

The site contains market overview statistics showing current activity, as well as current rules, regulations and other publications. There is a good deal of information about investing generally that will be of interest to many. Users can look up specific stock price quotes and can also track the progress of their portfolio, after entering some basic information. Again, a very important site, and a welcome addition to the Web for investors and others interested in securities.

Figure 12.7 *Ontario Securities Commission*
Figure 12.8 *Toronto Stock Exchange*

There is an excellent source of information from the OSC, however, in the form of The OSC Bulletin, a major publication for those who wish to keep up-to-date on securities matters. The bulletin is published by Micromedia, through their Web site at *http://www.mmltd.com*. A subscription is required of $500 per year per password to access the searchable database of all issues since January 1994. The system uses the popular Folio Views software. The bulletin is also available on CD-ROM and by email.

The BC Securities Commission has a great Web site at *http://www.bcsc.bc.ca*. It provides comprehensive information on securities regulation in that province, rules, decisions and hearings, and other related news items.

Both the Vancouver and Montreal Stock Exchanges have good, informative Web sites. The Montreal Exchange site at *http://www.me.org* offers interesting background on the mechanics of a stock exchange and also includes an excellent set of links to other exchanges in the world. The VSE site at *http://www.vse.com* contains notices, new listings, bulletins, and news releases, as well as copies of their policy and procedures manual and the rules and bylaws manual, both with searchable-text versions online.

There are innumerable sites available from sources outside of Canada, such as the New York Stock Exchange at *http://www.nyse.com*, Nasdaq at *http://www.nasdaq.com/welcome.htm* and many others. Of course the Securities and Exchange Commission (SEC) of the US has an excellent and comprehensive site at *http://www.sec.gov* providing much information of interest to investors and their advisors.

The SEC's Edgar site at *http://www.sec.goc/edgarhp.htm* has a well-developed site and is certainly worth bookmarking for those interested in companies falling under SEC rules. Edgar's Canadian counterpart, Sedar, also has a Web site at *http://www.sedar.com/homepage.htm*. This site has seen a tremendous expansion in the past year, and now contains the annual reports and other filing information of numerous companies in both Adobe (.pdf) format, which can be downloaded, and in HTML, which can be navigated easily on the Web site.

Another aspect of investor regulation is found in the role of the Canadian Investor Protection Fund which was set up to cover customers' losses of securities and cash balances, within prescribed limits, resulting from the insolvency of a member firm. The CIPF has a Web site at *http://www.cipf.tcn.net*. The CIPF is financed by members of the securities industry through the Sponsoring Self-Regulatory Organizations (SSROs)—the Toronto, Montreal, Vancouver, and Alberta Stock Exchanges, The Toronto Futures Exchange, and the Investment Dealers Association of Canada. When an investor becomes a customer of a member of any one of the SSROs, the accounts of that customer are covered by CIPF. The site provides extensive information about CIPF.

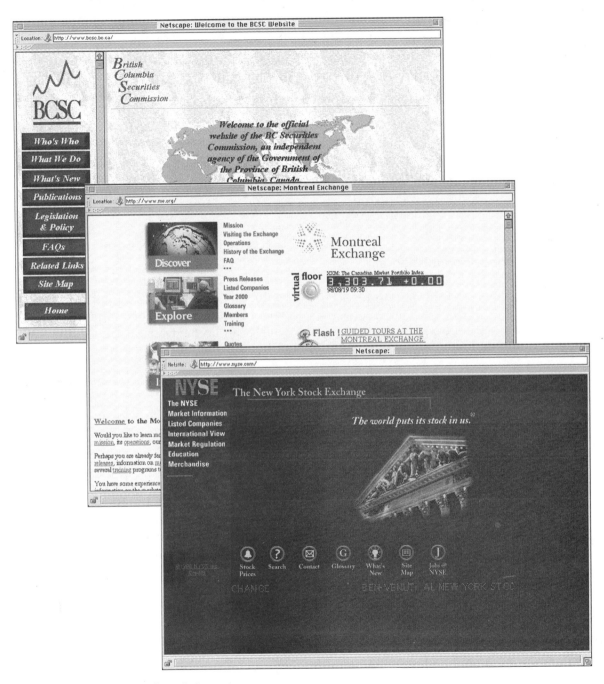

Figure 12.9 *BC Securities Commission*
Figure 12.10 *Montreal Exchange*
Figure 12.11 *New York Stock Exchange*

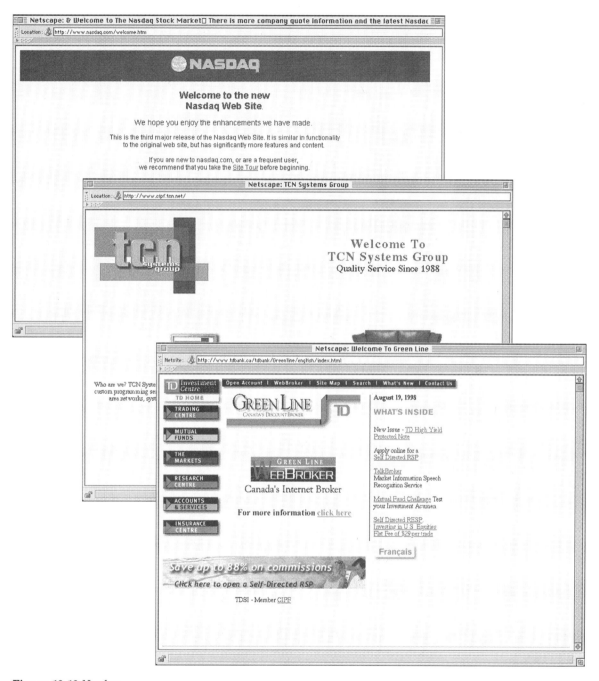

Figure 12.12 *Nasdaq*
Figure 12.13 *Canadian Investor Protection Fund*
Figure 12.14 *TD Green Line WebBroker*

INVESTING ON THE WEB

A phenomenon that has grown considerably in the past year or so is that of investing on the Web. Numerous sites now exist to facilitate buying and selling securities from the comfort of your own PC. This is done through the process of accessing online discount brokerage services. Of course, there are both advantages and disadvantages to the use of discount brokers. The big advantage, especially on the Net is convenience and low cost. The big disadvantage is that you are making investments completely without professional advice, and it is possible even for sophisticated investors to make serious mistakes without any consultation. However, the services are quite popular, and if one is careful and responsible, the discount brokerage services on the Net can be very useful, especially for managing self-administered RRSPs.

In the interests of simplicity, reliability, and security, we have concentrated our references here to those made available by the banks. No doubt, there are other safe and reliable sites, but we haven't sought them out.

- The Bank of Montreal offers a site called Investorline at *http://www.investorline.com /cgi-bin/Tango1.cgi/Investorline/ frame.qry?function=lr.*

- The Bank of Nova Scotia's Stockline Service can be found at *http://www.sdbi.com/ English/index.html.*

- Investor's Edge, a service of the Canadian Imperial Bank of Commerce, can be found at *http://www.cibc.com/products/ investment/invest_edge/.*

- The National Bank of Canada's online discount brokerage site is located at *http://www.invesnet.com/pbnIndex.htm.*

- The Action Direct service of the Royal Bank of Canada is located at *http:// www.royalbank.com/english/adirect/ netaction.html.*

- And finally, the pioneer among the banks of discount brokerage, the Toronto Dominion Bank, has an online site for its Green Line WebBroker at *http:// www.tdbank.ca/tdbank/Greenline/english/ index.html.*

SUMMARY OF WEB SITES MENTIONED IN CHAPTER 12

Name/Address

Canadian Financial Network Inc.
  http://www.canadianfinance.com

Bank of Canada
  http://www.bank-banque-canada.ca

Canada Investment and Savings
  http://www.cis-pec.gc.ca

Canadian Corporate News
  http://www.cdn-news.com

Infoglobe
  http://qsilver.queensu.ca/law/infoglob.htm

Bidding on Bay Street
  http://www.eucanect.com/investments/bayst.html

Gold Mining Stock Report
  http://www.infomine.com/newsletters/websites/gmsr.html

Hard Rock Analyst
  http://www.info-mine.com/hra

Winnipeg Commodities Exchange
  http://www.wce.mb.ca

Winnipeg Commodity Exchange quotes
  http://www.telenium.ca/WCE

Internet Financial Connection
  http://www.ifcstocks.com

Investors Guru
  http://home.istar.ca/~invguru

The Investors Newsletter Digest
  http://www.investorsnews.com

The Canadian Stock Market Reporter
  http://www.canstock.com

The Fund Counsel
  http://www.fundcounsel.com

The Business Development Bank of Canada
http://www.bdc.ca

Telequote
http://www.telequote.com

CBS MarketWatch
http://mw.dbc.com

Canadian Society of Technical Analysis
http://www.csta.org

The Canadian Home Builders Association
http://www.chba.ca

Canadian Association of Home Inspectors
http://www.bconnex.net/~jmlueck/cahi.html

CANNEX
http://www.cannex.com

Canadian Mortgage and Housing Corporation
http://www.cmhc-schl.gc.ca/cmhc.html

Chartsmart
http://www.chartsmart.com

Micromedia's Home Page
http://www.mmltd.com

US Securities and Exchange Comm
http://www.sec.gov

Ontario Securities Commission
http://www.osc.gov.on.ca

Toronto Stock Exchange
http://www.tse.com

BCSecurities Commission
http://www.bcsc.bc.ca

Nasdaq Stock Market
http://www.nasdaq.com/welcome.htm

New York Stock Exchange
http://www.nyse.com

Vancouver Stock Exchange
http://www.vse.com

Montreal Stock Exchange
http://www.me.org

EDGAR
http://www.sec.gov/edgarhp.htm

SEDAR Home Page
http://www.sedar.com/homepage.htm

Canadian Investor Protection Fund
http://www.cipf.tcn.net

The Bank of Montreal Investorline
http://www.investorline.com/cgi-bin/Tango1.cgi/Investorline/frame.qry?function=lr

The Bank of Nova Scotia's Stockline
http://www.sdbi.com/English/index.html

Canadian Imperial Bank of Commerce Investor's Edge
http://www.cibc.com/products/investment/invest_edge/

The National Bank of Canada
http://www.invesnet.com/pbnIndex.htm.

Royal Bank of Canada Action Direct
http://www.royalbank.com/english/adirect/netaction.html

Toronto Dominion Bank Green Line WebBroker
http://www.tdbank.ca/tdbank/Greenline/english/index.html

13 ELECTRONIC COMMERCE ON THE WEB

INTRODUCTION

In a broad sense, electronic commerce involves the carrying out of a business activity in an electronic form. It has been well underway in certain selected instances, such as Electronic Data Interchange (EDI) or Electronic Funds Transfer (EFT). It has also been conducted for some time through the use of linked corporate systems.

The growth of electronic commerce on the World Wide Web in the past year or so has been truly phenomenal. Although electronic commerce predated the Web with technologies like EDI, the Web could possibly dominate it in the long run. Ease of access, widely accepted technologies, and increasing effectiveness of security measures are all contributing to this trend.

The acceptability of Internet technology, such as TCP/IP, FTP, and HTML, has grown outside of the Internet, principally on private networks. This chapter begins with a description of some of the most common ways in which this is happening.

Various organizations have sprung up dealing with electronic commerce from many viewpoints. These include the Electronic Commerce Association (ECA) which has an extremely informative site at *http://www.eca.org.uk*. Another important global organization in this area is the Electronic Commerce World Institute with a site at *http://www.ecworld.org*. Other very useful sites from a practical viewpoint are CommerceNet at *http://www.commerce.net*,

the Electronic Commerce Canada Inc. Homepage at *http://www.ecc.ca/*, and the IBM CommercePOINT site at *http://www.internet.ibm.com/commercepoint*.

INTRANETS— SEAMLESS INTEGRATION

The term "intranet" has become the most common description of the use of internet technology on internal corporate networks. Intranets facilitate a "seamless" interface between the internal system and the Internet. In other words, the user is able to move freely and easily between the systems, perhaps not even being able to tell the difference between being on the Internet and on the home network.

Intranets can be on local area or wide area networks. Because internet technology inherently has poor security features, intranets are usually located inside a corporate firewall to try and prevent intrusion by unauthorized users.

WHY HAVE INTRANETS?

Intranets help to make communication with the world both feasible and cost effective. Since more powerful broadband communications systems are becoming available, and intranets tend to use them, performance improves. This includes the ability to handle audio clips and to stream (play while they download) sound and video files. The use of Internet technology makes sense because it is proven to be reliable and robust. In addition, it is being widely used, which means that new applications will tend to use that technology, assuring availability of compatible and cost-efficient applications. The cost of Internet technology, itself, is relatively low, compared to other proprietary systems.

THE USES OF INTRANETS

Intranets can be used for cost-effective publishing of corporate documents, like policy statements, manuals, brochures and directories. They can also be used to gain access to searchable directories, dealing with any variety of necessary information, such as product catalogues and price lists.

Since they look like the Internet, intranets can be used to post corporate, departmental or individual Web-type pages. At a

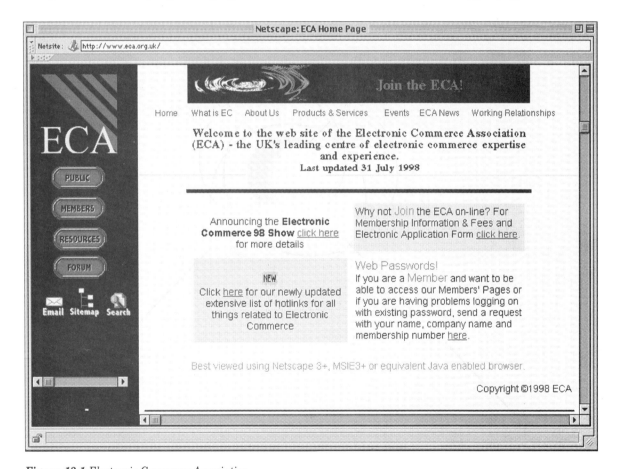

Figure 13.1 Electronic Commerce Association

practical working level, they can be used to apply simple groupware applications, to enable workers to collaborate on projects. They can also be used as an easy method for dissemination of software and, finally, they can be used for email—which can be fully compatible, indeed, the same as, Internet email.

The use of intranets has been growing rapidly in corporate networks. Increasingly, they will be used as the basis for business applications, because of their common interface with the world and their ability to be expanded (scaleability). As their use grows for commercial purposes, they are also being linked with the intranets of other organizations.

EXTRANETS– SELECTIVE INTEGRATION

The use of Internet technology to link private networks from different organizations gives rise to the creation of extranets. Such extended systems provide a link with suppliers, customers, and others sharing common goals. Unlike intranets, extranets extend outside the corporate firewall, but since they are specifically linked to another organization, arrangements can be made to make use of the

firewalls on the connected systems to design security for the system.

The advantages of extranets lie in their cost-effectiveness and their reliability. They can use existing Internet infrastructures and therefore are more economical than a proprietary network. Extranets enable trading partners, suppliers, and customers with common interests to form a tight business relationship and a strong communication bond. This is accomplished through sharing of information from each other's systems, and even the execution of selected transactions.

Examples of extranet applications include private newsgroups, groupware, training programs or sharing of other educational material, shared product catalogs, and project management and control for partnered companies.

The most significant aspect of extranets is that they are the first non-proprietary technical tool that can support rapid evolution of electronic commerce. They can be used to facilitate retail sales, credit cards, and various digital cash and payment settlement schemes and the global procurement of goods and services, all in electronic form.

A prime use of extranets is in the field of knowledge engineering. Data is gathered from suppliers, customers, and other key sources. Value is added by adding information to that data and disseminating (selling) the added-value product to the customers. Such "knowledge engineering" is a fundamental feature of the new information economy.

THE INTERNET–
GLOBAL
INTEGRATION

In one sense, electronic commerce on the Web is simply an extension of the use of extranets. The major distinguishing factor is that Web based electronic commerce involves a wider base of customers, not just those with interlinked systems. It can even involve the public at large.

An example of that was seen at the end of the last chapter, in the section dealing with online investing sites. Those are examples of transactional e-commerce sites. They involve transactions between individual investors and the banks (or their discount brokerage arms). The sites provided by the banks for online banking and bill paying are similar.

A large number of companies are using Web sites to conduct business transactions with their customers and to provide them with service. However, the use of the Internet for purposes of transacting business between companies has not been as visible, and perhaps not as fast-growing.

There have been a number of reasons expressed for inter-business electronic

commerce not growing as fast as one might think it should. The reasons appear to center largely around security and privacy issues. Consumers want to know that the site they are buying from is secure and that information being provided is kept confidential. In response to these and other concerns, a number of initiatives have been undertaken by various groups.

From an accountant's viewpoint, the most important initiative is that recently started by the AICPA and CICA. The WebTrust initiative is an assurance service that provides a graphic seal on client Web sites that meet the following three criteria:

1. business practices disclosure,

2. transaction integrity, and

3. information protection.

This initiative is discussed extensively at *http://www.aicpa.org* and at *http://www.cica.ca*.

Another initiative that is in place is through the National Computer Security Association (NCSA). Its site is located at *http://www.ncsa.com*. It promotes continuous improvement of commercial digital security through the application of the NCSA Risk Framework and NCSA Continuous Certification Model to certification, research, and related activities. NCSA is dedicated to continually improving global security, trust, and confidence in computing through the certification of products, systems, and people. NCSA Web certification is being promoted in Canada by SCI

Computer Security Canada Inc., which has a site at *http://www.csci.ca*. The company sees the program as the key to preventing security breaches in the financial industry.

Another organization involved in promoting trust and confidence in electronic transactions is TRUSTe. Their site is located at *http://www.etrust.org*. The principles behind TRUSTe are disclosure and informed consent: when users visit a Web site, they will be informed of what information the site is gathering about them, what the site is doing with that information, and with whom that information is being shared.

In addition, the approaches to encryption, authentication and certification are becoming more and more complex in an attempt to secure transactions and information. For example:

• Secure Electronic Transaction—Visa and Mastercard have developed the SET

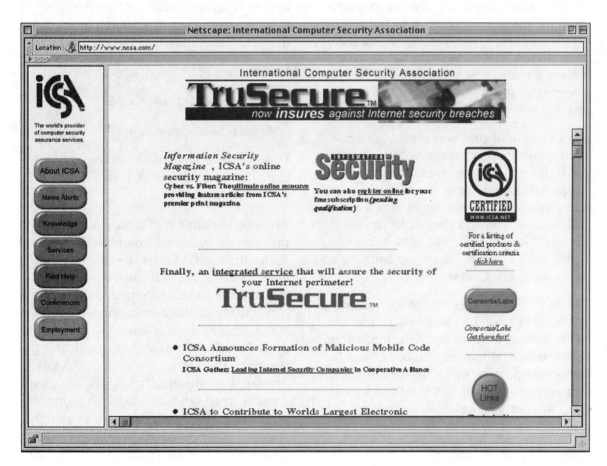

Figure 13.2 *NCSA National Computer Security Association*

standard with IBM for bank card payments over the Net.

- Secure Socket Layer (SSL)—contained in the current Internet browsers to send information between Web pages and browsers.

- Internet Protocol Security Standard (IPSEC)—a common technical standard on which security applications are being developed.

These are all initiatives that should promote consumer confidence in electronic commerce on the Web. The need for Internet security has caught the attention of many companies and commercial interests. Considerable action is being taken

- by vendors offering advanced security features and products,

- by users setting up more secure systems with firewalls and other security features, and

- by standards-setting bodies such as NIST, the OECD and other global organizations.

Java—Virtual Computing on the Net

One of the sources of security concern in certain quarters has been Java. This is the software developed by Sun Microsystems, with the initial intention to enhance Web pages using animation and powerful graphics capabilities.

Java first got the public's attention with its incorporation of applications that included stock tickers, sound, video, and cartoons in Web pages. But now it is becoming known as a computing platform—a base upon which software developers can build applications.

Many different kinds of applications can be developed using Java, including spreadsheets and word processors. In addition, and perhaps more significantly, mission critical applications can be built for both large and small companies—applications such as accounting, asset management, human resources, and sales.

Java applications, or applets, are different from ordinary applications in that they reside on a network server until they are called into use. Then the network delivers the applet to a user's computer or workstation when it is requested. For example, let's say you want to check your personal financial portfolio. You would dial into your financial institution and use your Web browser to log into the bank's system. The portfolio data would be shipped to you along with the applet needed to view it. Let's assume that you're considering moving your funds from one account to another, but first need to consider the pros and cons, such as fees charged and interest earned. There is no need to perform a series of cut-and-paste exercises. The system will send you an applet that will allow you to change the rate of interest and length of investment to perform a series of "what-if" scenarios.

Java simplifies the creation and deployment of applications, therefore saving time, resources, and money. Applications created in Java can be deployed without modification to any computing platform, therefore saving the costs associated with developing software for multiple platforms. And because the applications are stored on centralized servers, they eliminate the need to have users insert disks or CDs to update software. For all of these reasons, Java is being used extensively for conducting e-commerce transactions on the Web.

THE SECURITY CHALLENGE

JAVA

Java has presented some security challenges, which have been hotly debated in the electronic commerce world. Essentially, the Java people say that Java is a secure environment because the "applets" run in a "sandbox", and the sandbox is structured to prevent the applets from gaining full access to areas of the users' computer systems like the other files, programs, networks, and so on. They say the applet security manager runs the sandbox,

acting like a "playground cop". A description of the applet security policy is at *http://www.java.sun.com/sfaq.*

At present, some experts say that there is work to do in bringing Java up to a standard that would be fully acceptable for electronic commerce purposes, although this security situation is changing rapidly. Of course, Java is not the only area of the Internet presenting security issues.

ENCRYPTION

One of the other major areas of concern has been the encryption technology available. All sensitive security systems employ encryption and security standards are increasingly focusing on it. Indeed it has been argued that security cannot be achieved without adequate standards and technological capability for encryption.

In a paper issued in 1996 by the Clinton Administration, called "A Framework for Global Electronic Commerce", this importance is explicitly recognized. "Because cryptography is an important tool for providing computer security, the Administration has devoted a great deal of attention and effort to developing policies to promote the development and use of effective encryption products which encode both stored data and electronic messages".

In that paper, there also was mention of the fact that the administration "permits" companies to export encryption products using 56-bit Data Encryption Standard (DES) or equivalent algorithms for the next two years. The unstated "other side of the coin" is that the administration still restricts the export of DES products in excess of 56-bits, such as the stronger 128-bit technology. The degree of security in a DES product varies with the number of bits being used.

Recently, the Senate Commerce Committee passed a bill that advocates the use of a key based on the 56-bit algorithm. The fact is, the administration's policy, through its export restrictions, does not promote the use of DES technology. On the contrary, because of the growth of global

business and multinational enterprises, the policy restricts DES technology. Recently, it has allowed the export of high-end encrypted products to Canada, but at the time of writing, that is the extent of the exemption.

To compound the problem, there is mounting evidence that the use of a 56-bit DES technology is not enough in the world of the Internet. In mid-1997, a team led by Rock Verser, a freelance computer consultant, cracked the 56-bit DES

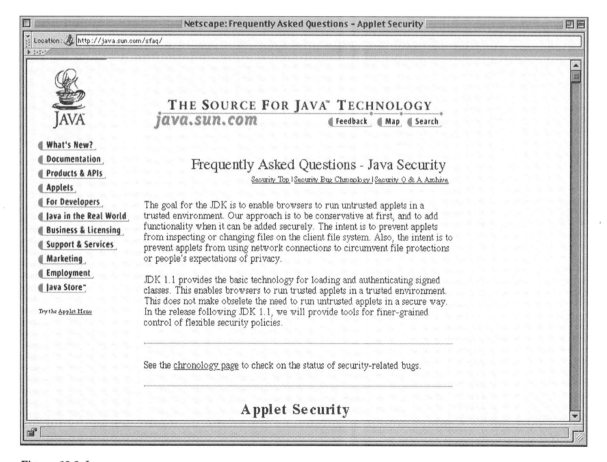

Figure 13.3 Java

encryption code. Verser had formed the "team" by sending out messages to the Internet asking people to download some keys and run them against a test program. Verser effectively used the power of the Internet to decode the DES algorithm, probably the biggest "brute force" code cracking exercise ever devised.

There are 72 quadrillion (72,057,594,037,927,936) possible keys in the 56-bit DES system. His 14,000 member team effectively tried about 18 quadrillion of them before coming across the right one.

Verser's project was in response to a challenge by RSA Data Security, offering a reward of $10,000 to crack the code. More information is available at *http:// www.rsa.com*. The purpose of RSA's challenge was to show the limited degree of security that the US government was allowing to be exported, and therefore the limited availablility of security to the global business community, of which a growing number of US companies are a part.

Financial institutions, who are the largest users of DES technology have been trying to compensate by using "triple DES", which places three DES operations back to back.

The US government is trying to foster the use of DES, but at the same time, restrict the availability of the most powerful DES products so it can have a better chance of decoding messages sent by organized crime, who are increasingly sophisticated in such matters. The concern is real, but the approach being taken, of restricting the availability of the most powerful DES technology, may well be hampering the growth of electronic commerce.

TUNNELLING

There are other methods being used to deal with the security limitations of the Internet. One of these is tunneling, which involves using the Internet as part of a private secure network. The "tunnel" is the particular path that a particular company message or file might travel through the Internet.

A protocol or set of communication rules called Point-to-Point Tunneling Protocol (PPTP) has been proposed that would make it possible to create a private network through "tunnels" over the Internet. Effectively, a corporation would use a wide-area network as a single large local area network. This would mean that companies would no longer need their own leased lines for wide-area communication but could securely use the public lines.

PPTP, sponsored by Microsoft and other companies, and Layer 2 Forwarding, proposed by Cisco Systems, are the basis for a new Internet Engineering Task Force (IETF) standard. With PPTP, which is an extension of the Internet's Point-to-Point Protocol (PPP), any user of a PC with PPP client support will be able to use an independent service provider (ISP) to connect securely to a server elsewhere in the user's company.

SOME CONCLUSIONS

It is clear that global business is expanding at a fast rate and that one of the prime enablers of this expansion is the use of technology. The result is that global business is increasingly electronic and electronic commerce is increasingly global.

It seems most likely that extranets will play an enhanced role in the growing world of business-to-business electronic commerce. They address many of the issues by enabling more control over the systems by the owners, not only from a security perspective, but also from an overall functional perspective.

It is well established that developers of new applications will direct their efforts to the platforms they most expect to be widely used, and therefore enhance the life of their product. At present many applications are being developed for Windows 95 because it is the most widely used operating system. In the new global electronic environment, applications will

Figure 13.4 RSA Data Security

be developed for Internet style technology, using Java and other Internet style technologies.

This will satisfy the need of business for a standard or uniform computing base. It will also set the stage for a growth in inter-enterprise computing. As the new systems become the standard, connecting numbers of organizations on common platforms, applications will be developed that will work on a uniform basis across organizational boundaries. The effect of this is difficult to overstate. It means that when companies adopt new systems they will do it on a cooperative basis so that their systems can run together. Instead, for example, of running a purchase module in one company and a sales module in the other, they will both be part of the same module including the purchase function of one company and the sales function of the other company.

Meanwhile, other events are taking place to change the environment wrought by the Internet. An important development has been the emergence of Internet II in the US. This is a new Internet, founded on the characteristics of the original Internet, which was used extensively for universities until it was discovered by the rest of the world.

A group of universities in the US is establishing Internet II to run on broad band pipes at 155 Mbps. The idea is that the capacity to convey huge amounts of data will enable multimedia streaming for classrooms and research. Multimedia streaming simply means that multimedia can be run on a system on a live basis. For example, if a video is to be played, it can be shown on the screen as the system receives it, rather than first downloading it and running an application to show it. This project is budgeted to cost US $100 million.

A similar project is underway in Canada through the assistance of the CANARIE consortium. Being similar to the US project, and given the high interaction between US and Canada, it is likely that the two projects will be linked, and perhaps the new systems as well.

Internet II will have an impact on the development of the existing Internet and whatever else follows the existing structures. It is unlikely that it will replace the Internet, but it is likely that the new world will see a world of many mansions where the the old Internet will still exist, largely in the form of a "freenet", and where there will networks of extranets, networks of internet tunnels and perhaps even various special purpose Internets, somewhat like Internet II.

Of this there is little doubt—the Internet will continue to evolve and grow into something very different than what we have now. But the basic idea of global networking is here to stay and the world will never be the same.

SUMMARY OF WEB SITES MENTIONED IN CHAPTER 13

Name/Address

Electronic Commerce Association (ECA)
   http://www.eca.org.uk/

CommerceNet
   http://www.commerce.net

Electronic Commerce Canada Inc. Home Page
   http://www.ecc.ca/

Electronic Commerce World Institute
   http://www.ecworld.org/

IBM CommercePOINT
   http://www.internet.ibm.com/commercepoint

International Computer Security Association
   http://www.ncsa.com/

NIST WWW Home Page
   http://www.nist.gov/

RSA Laboratories Home Page
   http://www.rsa.com

TRUSTe Home Page
   http://www.truste.org/

JavaSoft Home Page
   http://www.javasoft.com/

14 FINANCIAL REPORTING ON THE WEB

INTRODUCTION

In the past, many investors had to wait until the glossy annual report was received through the mail to read about a company's results for the year, its financial results, and plans for the ensuing period. This was often received months after the year end. Many corporations now release their annual reports to shareholders by way of the Internet.

BENEFITS

Use of the Internet is transforming the way many corporations release their results to the public. Corporations are now using the Internet to disclose either comprehensive financial statement data (the same as currently being disclosed in the annual report), summary financial data, or other corporate information to shareholders and potential shareholders. This not only reduces their overall cost (as fewer annual reports are being printed and mailed), but, more importantly, significantly reduces the time required to disseminate important information. Since the Internet is a dynamic vehicle of communications, as opposed to the old print media, investors have an opportunity to obtain much more up-to-date information by accessing information through the Internet.

Annual report information is released on corporate Web pages in two different for-mats—Adobe Acrobat (.pdf) format or in HTML. The difference is significant. Pdf files can only be read by using Adobe Acrobat, a text reader available on the Web, that preserves a high level of complex formatting. With this method, annual reports can be downloaded and read in the same format as the printed glossy report.

HTML, on the other hand, is designed to be read online, just like any other Web page. The Annual Report contains hyperlinks, so the reader can move around within the information quite readily. HTML pages can be downloaded, but not as easily as .pdf documents. The annual reports of many Canadian public companies are available on the Web page, (e.g., *http://www.sedar.com/homepage.html*), as discussed in previous chapters. Of course, the same information for US companies is found in the Edgar database at *http://www.sec.gov/edgarhp.htm* although EDGAR does not provide .pdf files.

EXAMPLES

It would be fruitless to try and identify all the financial reporting information sites. However, there are some general sites that are beginning to catalogue the companies that disclose annual report information on their Web sites.

A comprehensive site listing American companies is the Annual Report Gallery at *http://www.reportgallery.com/index.html.* This site provides links for similar sites providing annual reports from companies in other countries, such as Japan, Korea, and the UK. Another US site is the Annual Reports Library at *http://www.zpub.com/sf/arl* which offers extensive guidance on finding annual reports. The Annual Reports Library has built a collection of over 1.45 million original reports (and proxies) from corporations, foundations, banks, mutual funds, and public institutions. A site providing similar information for UK companies is CAROL found at *http://www.carol.co.uk.*

Other informative sites provide extensive information about corporate reporting, include the Micromedia Limited corporate info page at *http://www.mmltd.com/files/prod_serv/corp_inf/corpinf.html#cfi.* This site offers a guide to understanding corporate reporting, access to the Ontario Securities Commission bulletins, and a database of Canadian corporate reports. There is a fee for these services. Sedar provides the best

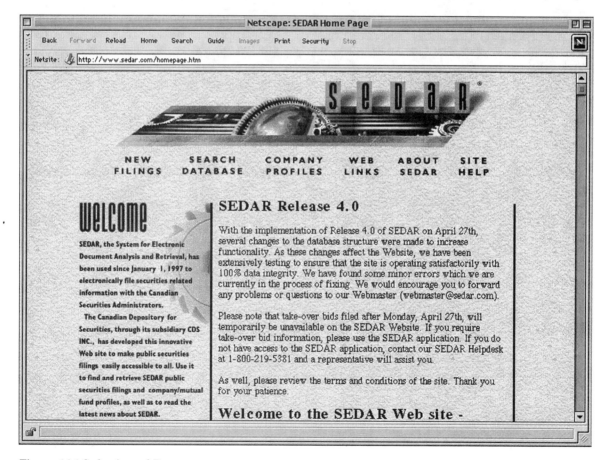

Figure 14.1 Sedar-Annual Reports

free source of Canadian corporate reports. Another site with excellent information about corporate reporting on the Web, including excellent papers discussing the issues, is that of the Summa project at *http://www.summa.org.uk...ucational*. Look under the Electronic Corporate Reporting link.

Following are some examples of the disclosures that can be found on Internet Web pages. This is a very, very small sam-

ple. In Canada, most public companies, such as, Bell Canada at *http://www.bell.ca/ bell/eng/about/invest/default.html*, Nortel at *http://www.nortel.com/home/home.html*, and Southam Inc. at *http://www.southam.com/ About/financialreports.html* provide comprehensive financial statement data on their Web sites. Others, such as Air Canada at *http://www.aircanada.ca/home.html*, Canadian Broadcasting Corp. at *http:// www.cbc.ca/aboutcbc/annualreport/ cbceng.html*, and TransAlta Corp. at *http://*

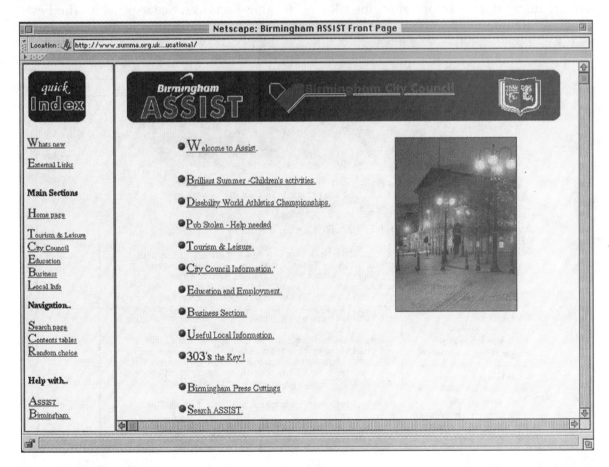

Figure 14.2 *Summa Project*

www.transalta.com/website/homepage.nsf? OpenDatabase provide highlights and/or news releases. This list changes daily.

Research done at Bradley University in Peoria, Illinois in 1996 showed that of the *Fortune 150* companies, 103 (69 percent) had Web sites, 48 had full comprehensive disclosure and another 27 had limited financial information available. It is reasonable to assume these numbers will continue to grow quickly.

CONCLUSIONS

Where will this all lead? Financial reporting is rapidly moving beyond the financial statements, as can be seen by much of the current research being done, and the advent of such vehicles of communication as the MD&A (Management Discussion and Analysis). The use of electronic means of disclosure, particularly disclosure on the Internet, is most likely to support and perhaps accelerate this trend, because of the vast array of information available on the Net and the many ways in which information can be linked.

It is expected that as financial disclosure continues to move beyond financial statements, it will place greater demands on auditors to provide an opinion on the data (so that the user might derive more confidence from the information). It is also likely, as the information being disclosed changes over time, that different reporting models will evolve to take the place of those currently in use. An example of such a development is the Business Reporting Model as set out in the report of the AICPA Special Committee on Financial Reporting, known as the Jenkins Committee. The report is on the Rutgers Accounting Web at *http://www.rutgers.edu/ Accounting/raw.html.*

SUMMARY OF WEB SITES MENTIONED IN CHAPTER 14

Name/Address

SEDAR
http://www.sedar.com/homepage.html

EDGAR
http://www.sec.gov/edgarhp.htm

Annual Report Gallery
http://www.reportgallery.com/index.html

The Annual Reports Library
http://www.zpub.com/sf/arl

CAROL
http://www.carol.co.uk

Micromedia Limited–Corporate Info page
http://www.mmltd.com/files/prod_serv/corp_inf/corpinf.html#cfi

Summa project
http://www.summa.org.uk...ucational

Micromedia Limited – Guide to Corporate Reports
http://www.mmltd.com/files/prod_serv/corp_inf/guide.html

Bell Canada
http://www.bell.ca/bell/eng/about/invest/default.html

Nortel
http://www.nortel.com/home/home.html

Southam Inc.
http://www.southam.com/About/financialreports.html

Air Canada
http://www.aircanada.ca/home.html

Canadian Broadcasting Corp
http://www.cbc.ca/aboutcbc/annualreport/cbceng.html

TransAlta Corp
http://www.transalta.com/website/homepage.nsf?OpenDatabase

Rutgers Accounting Web
http://www.rutgers.edu/Accounting/raw.html

INDEX